Published 10th December 2008,
the sixtieth anniversary of the
Universal Declaration of Human Rights,
by Camden Abu Dis Friendship Association (CADFA)

Designed by Ed Fredenburgh
Printed in Britain by Lightning Source

ISBN 978-0-9556136-1-6
EAN   9780955613616

اصوات
من
أبوديس

VOICES

FROM

ABU DIS

اصوات من أبو ديس

تحرير
ننيتا داوسن
عبدالوهاب صباح
جمعية صداقة كلمدن ابو ديس

This book is dedicated to the people of Abu Dis without whom of course it would not have been written; and to the many people in and around Camden who are working hard for the human rights of the people of Abu Dis and Palestine.

يهدى هذا الكتاب الى اهالي ابوديس الذين من دون مشاركاتهم لم يكون لهذا العمل ان يرى النوركذلك الشكر الجزيل للاصدقاء في كلمدن وحولها الذين يعملون بجد من اجل نصرة حقوق الانسان في ابوديس وفلسطين.

Acknowledgements

We would like to acknowledge with thanks the support of the **Barry Amiel and Norman Melburn Trust** for our project of collecting children's words, photos and pictures following the first Abu Dis children's visit to Camden in 2006. This book evolved from that project.

With many thanks to Ed Fredenburgh for his hard work on the design.

VOICES FROM ABU DIS

edited by
Nandita Dowson and
Abdul Wahab Sabbah

LIVING UNDER ISRAELI OCCUPATION

Introduction: 1948–2008   1

Living in Abu Dis: 4

SIXTY YEARS AGO	Abu Dis in 1948	6
REFUGEES FROM 1948	Our neighbour Sheikh of the Trees	9
1967: MORE REFUGEES	Forty years since the fall of Abu Dis	14
LOSING THE LAND	Land lost to the settlements	18
LOSING THE LAND	Child lost to the settlements	22
LOSING THE LAND	Land lost to the Separation Wall	24
LOSING THE LAND	New land confiscations	27
LOSING THE LAND	Report from Cllr Bassam Bahar	29
THE ENVIRONMENT	Rubbish dump and fears of cancer	31
THE ENVIRONMENT	The environment around Abu Dis	33
JERUSALEM	Al Quds past, present and future	36
THE SEPARATION WALL	Life in Abu Dis	40
THE WALL AND HEALTH	Forbidden to have a baby	42
THE WALL AND HEALTH	Born at a checkpoint	43
THE WALL AND HEALTH	My grandmother	44
THE WALL AND HEALTH	Blood transfusion	45
THE WALL AND HEALTH	Danger to the state?	46
THE WALL AND HEALTH	Killed at the checkpoint	48
THE WALL AND CHILDREN	I want my childhhod back	50
THE WALL AND CHILDREN	The separating Apartheid Wall	51
THE WALL AND CHILDREN	Voices from Abu Dis Boys' School	52
CHECKPOINTS, PASS LAWS	The Container checkpoint	54
CHECKPOINTS, PASS LAWS	Getting a permit for my grandfather	56
SEPARATED FAMILIES	Blue and green IDs	57
SEPARATED FAMILIES	Separating families	59
SEPARATED FAMILIES	Open Letter to UN Secretary General	61
ECONOMIC PRESSURES	A call for help	64
ECONOMIC PRESSURES	Out of work	65
PRESSURES ON EDUCATION	Studying at Al Quds University	66
PRESSURES ON EDUCATION	The army on the streets after school	68
PRESSURES ON EDUCATION	The army outside the school	69
PRESSURES ON EDUCATION	The army inside the school	70
PSYCHOLOGICAL PRESSURES	Al Marfa' Centre for Psychological Health	71
OCCUPATION VIOLENCE	Israeli soldiers on the rampage	73
OCCUPATION VIOLENCE	The martyr Fadi Baher	75
OCCUPATION VIOLENCE	The killing of Maryam Ayyad	76
MASS IMPRISONMENT	A present for Eid-al-Fitr	78
MASS IMPRISONMENT	My son in prison	80
MASS IMPRISONMENT	Arrested	81
DEMONSTRATION	Nakba march	83
POEM	Palestinian, you are not allowed to live	84

CONTENTS

CADFA work in Abu Dis   86

Letter to Camden Councillors   88
Letters from the schools   90
Women's Group at Dar Assadaqa, Abu Dis   92
To our friends in London   95
Support for my son   97
A letter to CADFA   98

Further information: how the national issues relate to Abu Dis   100

Refugees   102
Land confiscation and settlements   103
The Separation Wall   103
Israeli checkpoints   104
Israeli pass laws and Jerusalem citizenship   105
Mass imprisonment   106
Why do they call it apartheid?   107
Haiku on Israel's 60-years celebration   109

Resources   110

Maps   112
1   Shrinking Palestine   112
2   How the West Bank has been fragmented   114
3   The Wall   115
4   The area around Abu Dis   116
Timeline   118
Human rights   125
International Court of Justice ruling about the Wall   127
Where to find more information   128

Introduction

1948—2008

"I am surprised by this reservoir of sadness that is with me at the moment... I do not think I have ever been so profoundly moved by any life experience as much as I have been by the people of Abu Dis and the life they are forced to live" [1]

Sixty years ago this year, the United Nations agreed a Universal Declaration of Human Rights, recognising "the inherent dignity and ... the equal and inalienable rights of all members of the human family { as } the foundation of freedom, justice and peace in the world". [2]

It is also sixty years since the event that the Palestinians call the Nakba – a mass wave of refugees and the loss of three-quarters of their country to the new state of Israel [3].

This year, London is full of celebrations and commemorations as the history of that new state is feted on one side and brought to question by another; but in Abu Dis, in Palestine, neither of these sixty-year anniversaries bring any celebrations, because this has been sixty years of denial of their human rights.

Above left: 1948 – hundreds of thousands of Palestinians were forced from their homes into refugee camps like this

Below left: 2008 – hundreds of miles of Separation Wall wind through the West Bank (photo taken by Abu Dis children)

The events of 1948 left two areas of Palestine outside the new state of Israel: an area that came to be known as the Gaza Strip that came under Egyptian rule, and another that came to be called the West Bank which came under Jordanian rule. This included Abu Dis, originally a village on the hills next to Jerusalem, reputedly the site of Salah al-Din's encampment during the Crusades, and, by 1948, a suburb of the city and dependent on it, with its land stretching back east to the banks of the Dead Sea.

Britain's role in the creation of the current problems of Palestine goes back over ninety years to the Balfour Declaration and the partiality of the British Mandate [4]. As Britain prepared to wash its hands of the Mandate and turn Palestine over to the United Nations, the plan for Abu Dis, along with Jerusalem, was that it would be put into an area of international control [5]. But what followed was the war in 1948 and the declaration of the state of Israel on most of the land of Palestine, and Abu Dis joined the area that came to be known as the West Bank

NANDITA DOWSON

and came under Jordanian rule, until Israel took it in 1967.

1947-8 was a time of horror for the Palestinians: there was news of massacres in the west of Palestine with village after village demolished, major towns attacked and emptied of their Palestinian population. Uncounted thousands of people were killed and about half of the Palestinian population forced to leave their homes in the part of Palestine that became Israel [6]. They became refugees within and around the area, constantly hoping to return. Some of them moved to the area around Abu Dis.

The Nakba of 1948 remains important to people in Abu Dis, not just to the refugees, because to them it was a significant event in the pressure on Palestinians to leave their land that, they argue, started before 1948 and has gone on steadily ever since.

In 1967, when Israel occupied the West Bank and Gaza, hundreds of thousands more people were pushed from their homes and not allowed to return. And people still in Palestine feel they are still being pressurised to leave through systematic violations by the Israeli occupation forces of the human rights that the Palestinians, along with all of us, were promised by the United Nations sixty years ago.

Abu Dis

On a good day, a visitor to Abu Dis could find this small town slumbering in the sun, its people attempting to live a normal life, looking for work, studying, organising the lives of their big, close families, keeping in contact with far-flung friends on mobile phones and the internet. On such days, visitors look away from the Wall and the surrounding settlements and are charmed by warm, generous aspects of Palestinian society that are sometimes lacking in our own.

But as this book shows, Abu Dis is a town under military occupation by Israel, and the wounds from the occupation are never far away.

For the people of Abu Dis, normal life is constantly frustrated. Every family is living under tremendous

stress and uncertainty and has stories of suffering: separation, land expropriation, loss of family members, imprisonment, bullying by the Israeli army and the devastating construction of the Separation Wall.

What would you think?

Despite Britain's own role in the conflict, many in Britain have grown up with a very hazy understanding of the situation in the Middle East and wrong or stereotypical views of the Palestinians. (Because they suffered from it, people in Palestine remember Britain's role with greater vividness than many people in Britain do.)

But the work of Camden Abu Dis Friendship Association is based on a belief that if ordinary people in Britain understand the human lives of the people of Palestine and compare them to their own lives, they can play a strong role in demanding for them the same things we want for ourselves: respect, freedom and human rights.[7]

CADFA therefore makes links of many sorts between people and organisations in Camden, London and in Abu Dis, Palestine. And as these links strengthen, we are often asked for more information about the situation and people's daily lives.

This book is one way of giving that information [8]. These are typical stories from people's lives that have been sent to CADFA during the past four years. They show something of what life is like for the people of Abu Dis, 60 years after the Nakba and over 40 years after the Israeli occupation of the West Bank, Gaza and Jerusalem.

We hope that the stories will motivate people to find out more, and also to want to do something to help. They are followed by some of the comments by people in Abu Dis about CADFA's work that encourage us to keep going. The information at the back of the book is included to encourage you to be active with CADFA and other groups who work to promote human rights in Palestine.

FOOTNOTES

[1] Letter from a CADFA volunteer returned from Abu Dis, 2008

[2] www.unhchr.ch/udhr/

[3] Ilan Pappe *The Ethnic Cleansing of Israel*, 2007

[4] ibid

[5] United Nations Partition Plan 1947—United Nations Resolution 181—see map page

[6] Ilan Pappe, 2007

[7] An illustration of this sort of comparison is the photomontage *[below]* made by 14-year-old Adam in response to stories of Abu Dis told by a CADFA visitor

[8] You can find further information on our website or from contact@camdenabudis.net

CADFA also organise visits to Palestine and Abu Dis and arranges visits from Abu Dis. See our website for forthcoming opportunities to meet people from Abu Dis in Camden.

Living in
Abu Dis

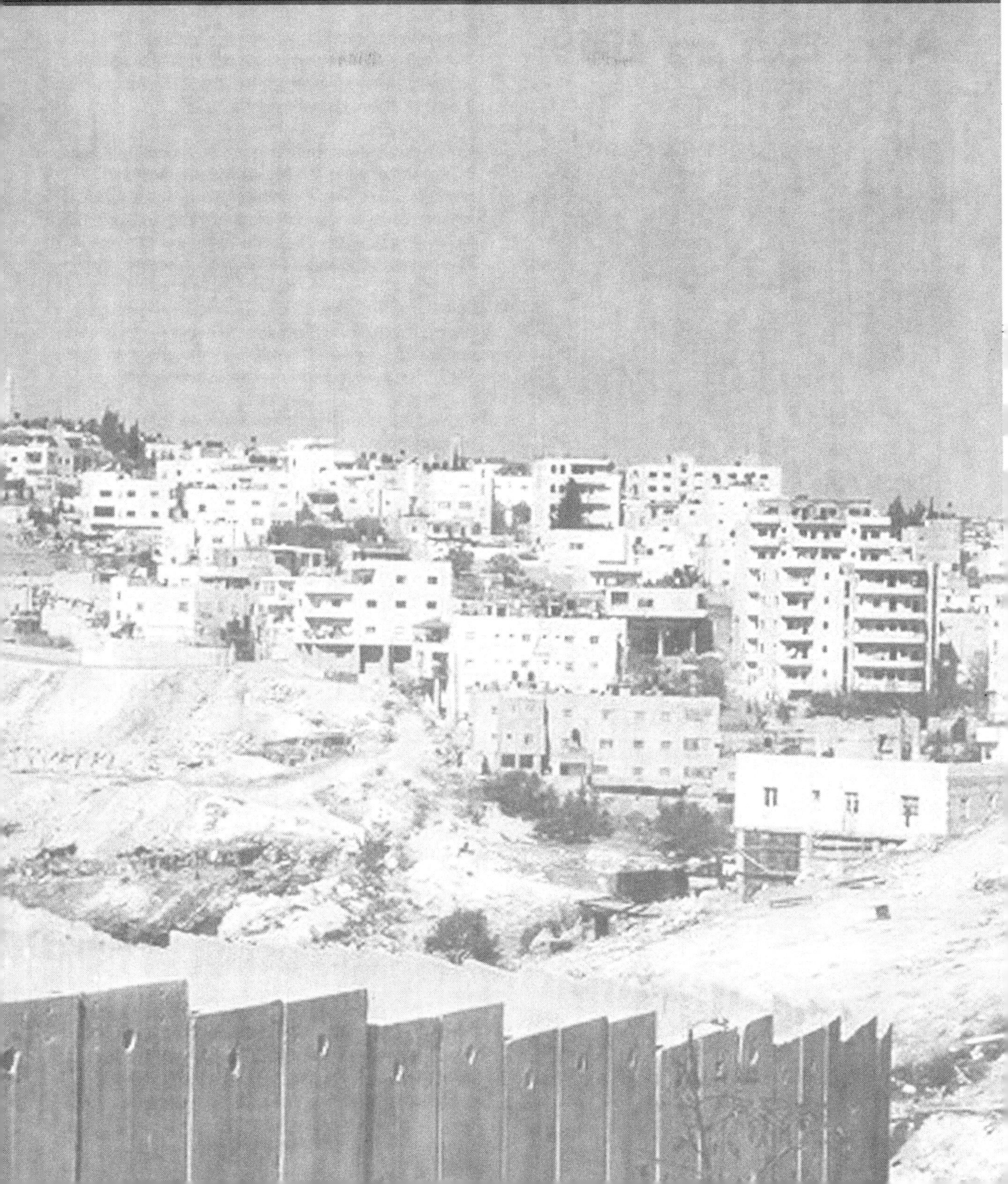

Abu Dis in 1948

YUSSUF AYYAD, 2008

Abu Dis people call him Yussuf al-Haj.
He is now 75 years old

Of course I remember life in Abu Dis around 1948. The main thing I remember all my life is the land and working on my land- this is the only thing I can do and it is what I have done all my life.

Before the first war between the Arabs and the Jews [1], my father used to take me together with my brothers to our land. I can't even count how much land because we used to own hundreds of donums on the east side of Abu Dis, from Wadi Abu Hindi south of Abu Dis reaching to Al Nabi Mousa in Jericho area.

The main things we used to grow were wheat and barley, beans and chickpeas.. We used to own sheep and goats – just as all Abu Dis people did at that time. My father used to own more than a thousand.

As for food, everything came from our land. We used to depend on bread, jreeshi [2] and maftoul [3]. We did not eat as much rice as people do now, and if we had it, we had to buy it in Jerusalem or in Jordan.

Abu Dis used to be a small town, stretching from Al Ras neighbourhood to the old market near the mosque. There were about 4000 people in Abu Dis at that time. Each house in Abu Dis used to have sheep, cows and chickens. There were three shops owned by Al Haj Hussein Shahad Ayyad, Al Haj Hussein Ali and Al Haj Mustafa Ayyad – my father. The main things they sold were meat and flour.

At that time, Abu Dis was very well-known for having sheep – it had the largest number of sheep in the Jerusalem area. About fifty people from different families in Abu Dis used to go into Jerusalem on donkeys every day. I used to go with my mother. We delivered milk to different neighbourhoods in the city. If any Abu Dis person did not take their milk to Jerusalem, there would be a whole extended family in Jerusalem who stayed without milk that day. We also sold milk at Damascus Gate market. Abu Dis people also sold milk in Bethlehem and cheese in Jordan.

At harvest time, nobody from Abu Dis used to stay in the village. Everyone—women, children, men—used to go to the east side of Abu Dis to bring in the harvest. The women used to cook for everybody and to send food, rice or jreeshi to the fields and the houses for the people who did not have it. It was a very strong community in those days.

In Abu Dis there was only one midwife to help women have babies. She was Sheikha Shehadeh Ayyad. Even Hospice Hospital in Jerusalem did not deal with childbirth so the only thing was to use midwives. Sheikha Shehadeh Ayyad was very famous then like your ambulance is now. A very high percentage of babies died just after birth because there was no health care. In my own family, out of thirteen babies that we had, not one survived beyond babyhood.

At that time, there were two buses that took people from Abu Dis to Jerusalem. There were no streets in Abu Dis. People used to walk to Kubsa if they wanted the bus, so it was easier to walk the whole way to Jerusalem and not wait for the bus. We used to go to Jordan by bus – it took one and a half hours.

In 1948,[4] there was a police station belonging to the Arab army. One time I went to Jerusalem to buy some shoes, and I bought some second-hand boots. I was very happy to have new shoes. So I put them on and I decided to walk back home as usual. The policemen in that police station saw that they were old army boots and they had a mark on them showing that they belonged to the army, so they arrested me. My father had to pay money for me or I would have had to stay in jail for 15 days.

Although the majority of people in Abu Dis at that time were farmers, there were people who worked all over Palestine, in Acre and Haifa, often preparing the stones for building.

At that time, the whole Jerusalem area used to be one area: the people from the city and the surrounding villages used to depend on each other. People from Abu Dis went into town with milk and agricultural products, and people from the city—from al Tour (on the Mount of Olives) or Silwan—used to come to build houses for people in Abu Dis, but they used to cut the stones from Abu Dis itself.

Things that happened – There were three women from Abu Dis killed in 1947. That happened in Damascus Gate when my mother was selling milk with the other Abu Dis women. Jewish terrorists threw a container of explosives at a crowd of people in the market there. One of the people died was was Fatmeh al-Haj from the Ayyad family.

The traditional habit in Abu Dis is that families support each other at times like this. So that day, the Badr family cooked for the Ayyad family because they were arranging a funeral, but at that time they didn't know that a member of their own family, Mohammed Abdullah Badr, had gone to the Dome of the Rock and he was shot and killed on the very same day.

In 1948 some Abu Dis people were among the Palestinian fighters but they used to work in the areas of 1948, not locally [4]. After the 1948 war, there were lots of refugees from West Jerusalem arriving in Abu Dis, and the Zionist gangs chased the refugees right up to Abu Dis. The Zionist gangs made a checkpoint in Kubsa [5]. They used to allow people through to Abu Dis but not let anyone go out of it to Jerusalem. They told them that if they returned west they would be killed.

The refugees came to Abu Dis and of course the people in Abu Dis welcomed them but there was no space to have them in the houses, so many of them stayed in local caves. Refugees told us about the very big and beautiful houses they had built in Al Bakaa and Katamoun and Ifta but they did not even manage to live in them because the Zionists took them.

Many families shared land and harvest with them and tried to help them. Soon they became part of our community. ·

FOOTNOTES

[1] 1948

[2] cracked wheat: people make a salty, yoghurty sauce

[3] rolled wheat and semolina, like couscous but bigger grains

[4] the areas of Palestine that became Israel in 1948

[5] the part of Abu Dis near Aizariyeh, on the main road to Jerusalem

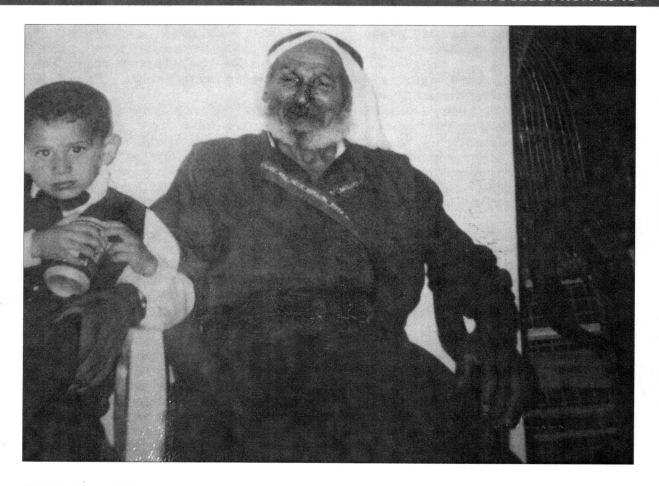

**Sheikh Ahmed Mansour Imam, may he rest
in peace**

Our neighbour Sheikh of the Trees

The Sheikh was born in the year 1932 in the village of Souba, one of the villages on the west of beautiful Jerusalem . He lived the first part of his life there with his parents and his brothers and sisters. They tilled the land and grew soft fruit, fruit trees and vegetables, because that was a fertile place and there were springs of water there. There was a link of love, affection and dreams between them and their land.

But soon the love was destroyed and the dream was stolen with the events of the Nakba of 1948, when news came of the massacre at Deir Yassin and Al Shayat. Stories were told about how people were forced from there and the villages near to the war, fearing for their children and for their land, which had been spoiled there. At that time, Sheikh Ahmed was sixteen years old, and he left, along with his family and all the people leaving from the places of 48, hoping to return after 15 days. This then became a month and then stretched to six months and he didn't know that the wait would stretch to his whole life.

Some of them went to the area of Aizariyeh and the family of Sheikh Ahmed settled in Abu Dis. After a time, the United Nations Relief and Works Committee set up a project in Aizarieyeh called Shelter for the Refugees, and the family of the Sheikh were first housed in a cave, then in a small hut, and issued with an UNWRA card. They survived on food handouts that were distributed to them and second-hand clothes passed on from America. They found some work from the families of the village. The women embroidered dresses for the women of the area and to tell the truth they were good at everything they turned their hands to; and if anyone looked properly they would see in what they did the flat, fertile places of the Palestinian plains and the hurt and pain of its people.

A link of friendship grew between them and the families of the village. And Sheikh Ahmed was respected by everybody despite his simplicity and limited means. He married a woman from Kastel called Miriam Mateer, but they couldn't have any children at first. He told me that there was no traditional medicine or remedy that they did not try.

NAJAH AYYAD, 2008

The Sheikh had to find some sort of employment to live from, and also to pay for the costs of medicine. He looked for a job but there was nothing in his heart but land and trees. He owned a donkey and so he started to plough and cultivate the land for other people in summer and winter seasons, and he was excellent at what he did, better than an agricultural engineer. His reputation spread and he became famous in the local villages in the hilly area of Abu Dis, Sawahreh, Al-Tour, Aizariyeh and Silwan, the villages of East Jerusalem.

Abu Hamza

After seven years of treatment, at last they had their first child, Fatima; then Ibrahim, then Waleed. They brought them a lot of joy. They loved people and they were loved by them; they shared their joys and sorrows and everybody wished them well.

He was called by people the Sheikh of the Trees. He really deserved that title and if there were justice on earth he would be the owner of the whole plain of Latroun.

I knew him from the year 1994 when we were building our new house next to their house…I had been away from the country for a long time so I felt like a stranger. We had a house near Aizariyeh and we also loved the land, specially after living cooped-up in a flat in Riyadh which created a longing for the land. We were always dreaming of returning and building a country house and planting all kinds of trees and vegetables and we wanted to garden and harvest and build a place for chickens.

And when we became neighbours and found that our dream and his dream coincided, really there was a huge closeness between us and his family … He used to come and sit with us in the garden and drink tea with mint or with sage harvested from the land that we had worked on together and developed together… He told us about Souba, and its springs and its soft red earth and how he worked the land with his father and raised goats and gathered wild plants like sage and green thyme … and the beauty of nature there and the delicious figs… and the dew at night… and the sound of the wind and the yellow leaves in winter… and the roses and poppies in spring… On every visit he would tell us stories, and bring us small plants of flowers or vegetables or saplings of trees at the time of pruning. We told him to think of our land as his own.

He told us that people had offered him a lot of land to use and to build a house on, and after the Naksa of 1967, he had been invited to live in the house of one of the families who had left and gone to Jordan but he had refused. He said "My eyes are on Souba. I want to go back and I want to be buried there." – That was his firm wish.

How generous and proud he was. If someone gave him a bite, he would return a whole dish. He used to take care of all the land that he worked on as if it were his own land. But his eyes were always on Souba.

A story that he told. After the 1967 war, he managed to visit Souba. He saw their land and it was surrounded by a fence, and planted with various special types of fruit, because of the quality of the land. He asked a Jewish man if he could come and see the land, but he refused him and instead told him roughly to go away: "Yallah – Get going."

He left in deep pain and sorrow.

A story. Before 1948, there were Jewish terror attempts to strike fear in the hearts of people and force them to leave their houses. Once he was tending the sheep with his brother near Rafa spring and the Jews threw bombs at them. The boys lay on the stomach near the ground and the bombs fell near them but didn't explode. But similar things harmed other people.

Finally the family built a simple house, but they didn't develop it, thinking they would return home.

Souba village

Once we woke up in the morning and we saw from the window- to our amazement – an askidunia tree [1], covered in fruit. I asked my husband what it was, and he was surprised and said "In the name of God! Who put that there?" The Sheikh called out from below, "I'm down here."

His children grew up. Ibrahim studied in Ibrahimi College and married a girl from West Sawahreh who had a blue ID. They had three boys and a girl. In 1998, Im Ibrahim [2] got ill and became disabled. She fell and broke her hip. The Sheikh and Fatima stayed looking after her until she died on 24th February 2000.

Fatima told another story. When the Naksa of 1967 happened [3], the Sheikh and his wife left and took Fatima to Jordan. They didn't stay long, and managed to come back quickly, but Fatima didn't go to school because her mother was scared for her – particularly as she had been born after a long period of wanting to have a baby – and because of the feeling of being alien, away from their own place. When they returned to Abu Dis, her mother wrote a letter to the school and Fatima stayed without education.

At the time when the mother's illness became severe, Waleed got married. He married a girl from Hussan in summer 2000, and at the time of writing they have two girls and a boy.

After the death of his wife, the hope of returning weakened for the Sheikh, and after the Jenin massacre, the Sheikh was hit by diabetis. He did not keep up with the medication so his illness developed in stages, up to the point when, in 2006, he lost his sight. He stayed patient and went to the mosque and prayed. Thank God he could actually tell who was near him, and he refused to hold anyone's hand. I don't know where he got this greatness after all his misery.

One day he fell on the ground and injured himself and had to stay in bed. Again it was Fatima who looked after him. In his last days, he couldn't reach the bathroom alone, the injury on his foot made his condition worse, and he developed a sore that would not heal.

He was always calling for us; he loved our kids and they loved him. Our son Hamza was in the course of his training at a health centre in Aizariyeh and he used to visit him. Abu Hamza [4] used to go to see him when he came home from work. He was still talking about his village and his days there, even when he was very ill.

One day Hamza came home in the mid-afternoon and told me that the Sheikh was extremely ill, and asked what he should do? The Sheikh's children were at work and so were his other relatives. We rushed by car and Hamza took him to the doctor and he was right away transferred to hospital. He was really suffering. We took him through the checkpoint.

The doctor said his leg should be amputated, but the Sheikh refused. He said that, even if the badness spread through his body (he had gangrene) he wanted to die with his body complete.

He returned home and the illness spread rapidly through him, and at about six in the morning on 28th March 2007, he died, God rest his soul.

That wasn't the end of the story. The Sheikh used to dream of returning to Souba. Time passed and he didn't return. He hoped to return, even if in a coffin to be buried in the kind earth. This dream was not realised, it was impossible. In the difficult circumstances of the country, he had more recently said, "If I can't be buried in Souba, let me be buried in Jerusalem."

After the beginning of the Separation Wall, it became impossible for anyone without a Jerusalem ID to go to Jerusalem, even if for a funeral. The Sheikh's two sons are divided from each other – one with a green ID and one with a blue one. His other relatives were also divided in this way.

The Sheikh's last words were "Bury me in Jerusalem," and they decided to honour them even though they knew from their experience that it was well-nigh impossible to take him through the terminal.

The Sheikh would have been happy for ever to realise that this dream of his lifetime was realised.

There was an English woman guest in Abu Dis who learned of the story and wanted to accompany the funeral and see what happened. When they got to the Zeitunah terminal, the soldier refused to let them enter, and stopped the funeral. Some of the people with it passed through the checkpoint and some were left behind. The English woman started to take photos of the checkpoint and the soldier wanted to stop her doing that. While he was busy with that, the people carrying the body went very quickly and put it in a car – this was possible because the Sheikh had become light during his illness, which helped them to carry him. The car quickly passed through the checkpoint towards the cemetery at Bab al-Ispat and the other car returned to Abu Dis.

The soldier looked at the woman and asked where the dead man was. She laughed and said, "He ran away." She went on after the funeral, but did not know where the cemetery was. But luck was the ally

of the funeral in the end – the Sheikh got to Jerusalem and was buried there, even if not in Souba.

Possibly there are doubts about the truth of this story – but there were witnesses, and the strongest evidence is that his grave is there.

FOOTNOTES

[1] Loquat tree

[2] Im Ibrahim – Ibrahim's mother, the Sheikh's wife

[3] This is the name given to the 1967 Occupation

[4] Abu Hamza – Hamza's father, the author's husband

The Wall being built

Forty years since the fall of Abu Dis

INTERVIEWS WITH REFUGEES FROM ABU DIS, NOW LIVING IN JORDAN

RASHA ABDULLAH SALAMEH, 2008

Left: Abu Dis refugees on the road to Jericho, 1967

She is leaning her tired body on the same wall she has leant on for 40 years while she hums the folk song which she has never forgotten, "You who are passing through Abu Dis, stop and see, we have youth in the main square and sugar on the shelves." Her lifelong friend takes over with a stronger verse about the hospitality of Abu Dis: "Three villages without a breath of wind to give you, Al-Tour, Silwan and Aizariyeh; turn to Abu Dis, they will pour you ghee and custard."

The two old ladies, Hajeh Zareefeh al-Baow, and Hajeh Mashayikh Jaffal still keep the scent of their peaceful Jerusalem village Abu Dis after four decades of the occupation, and after the majority of its people left it, as happened with the other villages and towns in Palestine, fearing the Israeli attacks.

With hopeful looks that haven't faded over the decades, Hajeh Zareefeh says: "Abu Dis had open arms for refugees in the year 1948. We were all family, people came to us from Deir Yassin and Beit Jeez and from Al Kastel and from other villages as well. Everyone in Abu Dis had plenty, and everybody welcomed them warmly, which is why these rhymes were made up." (She is explaining the rhymes above.)

Hajeh Mashayikh picks up a thread of secret sadness, and says "Palestinians were not allowed to carry weapons in 1948. The British were put in control of us and when they went out they delivered Palestine to the Jews."

Sighs of pain came with their recollections. Tears came from Hajeh Zareefeh's eyes and the strong memories of Abu Dis did not stop them. She said, "When the war started, we were very afraid, and we imagined it would be just some days and we would return to Abu Dis. Even after we were defeated, we were sure that it would be a story of some months, and everyone would return back home. But the years passed and we are still waiting to go back."

She stopped for a while, trying to catch her breath, and she said, "When we went out of Abu Dis, it was very tragic .. shock and fear and sadness ... We just took some basic things and whatever food we had saved in the caves next to our houses, and we just left."

With deep sorrow in her voice, Hajeh Zareefeh said, "My cousin, Ahmed al-Baow was helping his wife, his children and his in-laws to cross the river Jordan. And when they reached the middle of the river, the Israelis started shooting at them. They killed the whole family in front of his eyes. Right up to now he is hoping to find one of his children, hoping that they might not all be dead."

Hajeh Zareefeh started to cry very hard, while Hajeh Mashayikh tried to support her, as she had done in all the past years, and she took over from her, saying: "My son was in Egypt in his first year at university at the beginning of the war. My heart burned when I heard his voice on the radio. He said 'My name is Abdullah Mohsen, I just want to reassure my family in Abu Dis that I am in good health .' "

With a sigh of brokenness that is still fresh till today, she went on: "At that moment I felt that I was very weak, because we had lost the war, and my son was away from me, and we were here in the middle of nothing, and nobody knew what had happened to the others. Death was better than these moments."

The bitterness of a wound that had not healed in forty years has not left Hajeh Zareefeh. She was feeling the embroidery on her Palestinian village dress that she, like her friend, still wears after all these years, as they used to in their calm village: "Abu Dis and all Palestine was like heaven for us – wheat, barley, kersanah [1], figs, grapes, apricots, olives and wells of water."

There was grief in the voice of Hajeh Mashayikh who said, "Abu Dis is all beautiful, but the most beautiful place is Al Marj, and the areas of al-Rukbeh and Sha'ib and al-Mrussuss, which is the area that the Jews stole and where they built Maale Adumim settlement. Abu Dis was snuffed out like a candle."

Hajeh Zareefeh was wringing her hands with grief when she said, "When I saw photos from Abu Dis, I was so so sad. The Israelis have killed Abu Dis with the Apartheid Wall that they have built. Abu Dis used to stand for fresh breeze and bright atmosphere; we used to see the Dome of the Rock from our village … Today Abu Dis is under occupation, nobody will give it the care and love that we did …"

Tears came from the eyes of Hajeh Mashayikh when she said, "May God never forgive them for taking us out of our land and scattering us across the world. Each of my children is in a different country, still strangers wherever they are, long years after what happened to us." Hajeh Zareefeh interrupted her and said, "Also my children, each one of them is in a different country, and my heart breaks when I hear them remembering Abu Dis and saying that they can go all over the world but they can't reach their own land."

The old town of Abu Dis

And like the open arms and the great shade of Abu Dis, Hajeh Zareefeh and Hajeh Mashayikh hug their grandchildren who don't stop asking about Abu Dis and the weddings that brightened the evenings, and the days when they had plenty, repeating "What crime did we commit that all of that had to be taken away from us?"

FOOTNOTE

[1] *Kersanah* – a cereal crop

Land lost to the settlements

I was born in 1930. My family owned 90 donums in the area of Sha'eb Abu Suwan which the Israelis have now made into Maale Adumim settlement. Now, the Israelis have changed my land and made it into a sports field and a garden. I take my children and my cousins to the different places in east Abu Dis and point out to them the land they can see, so they know where their land is.

In Wadi Abu Hindi, my family owned about 50 donums. The Israelis made that land into a closed security zone and then they built a road across it connecting Maale Adumim settlement with Qidar settlement. I know the area well and I want my sons and grandsons to know the land exactly, because I believe that rights don't disappear with time and it will be important that there is somebody who knows the land who can claim it.

My family also owned 2 donums at Araq al-Ameer and 6 donums in the area of Dinar, where Qidar settlement was built, and another 8 donums in the area of Al Hadab which is an area where there are now temporary caravans where Israeli settlers live while they are preparing to build houses in Old Qidar.

When I was a child, the family used to survive well on the produce of this land: for the whole year, we had enough.

Starting in 1942 when I was twelve, I used to go regularly with my father to our land. We used to work to grow crops – corn and okra and cucumbers and wheat. In the season before the harvest, I used to sleep there with my father, sometimes for more than a week. We did shifts to stay awake to make sure that the birds and the animals did not eat the ripe crops.

After my father died in 1953, my family rented the land to another family in Abu Dis in exchange for a share of the crops, which helped us to survive. In that period, we did not need to go to the shop: we used to get everything from that land, bread, corn, vegetables, everything.

We used to pay taxes to the Turkish and even to the British, and we still have the receipts for the taxes we paid for our land to the British.

The land has been changed a lot by the Israelis but

MOHAMMED AHMED AFANEH, 2008

I can identify exactly where it is, because the small church that was built on Jaffal land was exactly by our land.

The Israelis started building Maale Adumim settlement in 1976. There were big demonstrations against the settlements in Abu Dis. The boy Ali Afaneh was killed by the Israeli army on one of those demonstrations.

Our land was on the north side of the settlement – there was no building, nothing on it, but the Israelis took it over as a military settlement.

In 1983 the Israeli bulldozers started to work on the land. Before that it was a small valley with hills, but the Israelis filled it with earth, they levelled it for a sports field. Abu Dis people did not accept that, and there were demonstrations in 1983, and I was one of the people who joined in those demonstrations.

The Israeli military leader who was in charge of the area came to meet with the mukhtars [1] – there were three mukhtars in Abu Dis at that time, one from each hamouli [2]. He did not give them any official document or military decision on the future of the land, but he just told them that from now on, their land was not for them: it was a closed military area.

FOOTNOTES

[1] These were the old village leaders

[2] Clan

Two of the illegal Israeli settlements built on Abu Dis land

Below left: part of Maale Adumim – one of the biggest of the settlement blocks in the West Bank

Below: Qidar settlement, which is currently being extended

Child lost to the settlements

FROM WITNESS STATEMENTS FROM ABU DIS

In 1976 there were big protests in Abu Dis against the beginning of the building of the settlement of Maale Adumim on the land of Abu Dis and Aizariyeh. During one of the demonstrations, young people from the secondary schools in Abu Dis went to the main street in Aizariyeh which was the road that the settlers used at that time to get from Jerusalem to the new settlement. (Now they have a different road and this historic road is blocked by the Separation Wall).

One of the boys on this demonstration was Ali Afaneh who was aged eleven.

Two settlers came in a military jeep and they shot at the children. They hit Ali twice in his head at a distance of about ten metres. They also wounded two girls from Abu Dis Girls' School. After they shot Ali, they took him in their jeep to the Hadassa Hospital on the Mount of Olives, on his own.

Below: Ali Afaneh in hospital

Below right: Ali's sister points to the place where he was shot

People from the area (Al-Tour) were there when Ali arrived at the hospital. They told the family that the settlers let him fall out of the jeep on to the ground while the jeep was still moving, and that his clothes were caught by the jeep, so he was pulled along the ground for some time by his clothes.

He was kept in the hospital for three weeks. The family went often to see him but they were kept away from him, behind glass, and they are sure that he had died before that. After three weeks, the family were forced to pay for the hospital treatment.

Then there was an issue about how his body was to be returned to the family. Witnesses tell how Israeli soldiers came to the house and searched it, looking in particular for cameras or people from the media.

Usually there would be a funeral procession from the house to the funeral, and so they waited for Ali to be brought to the house, but the Israeli military put a curfew on Abu Dis to ensure everyone stayed indoors, and they brought his body back at night, and took him straight to the cemetery.

They allowed his mother and his aunts to bury him, but his father and the other men were forced to stay inside.

Below left: Ali's family waiting to receive his body

Below: Ali Afaneh as his family like to remember him

The Mourners Wait

The bereaved parents, brothers and sister of 10-year-old Ali Hussein Afana waited in Abu Dis, a town in the Israeli-occupied West Bank of the Jordan, for the boy's body to be released to them. Moslem tradition calls for burial before sundown, but the family waited anxiously as night fell and no word had been received from Israeli authorities. The youth was fatally wounded last week by Israeli gunfire during anti-Israel demonstrations in the West Bank.

Land lost to the Separation Wall

Jamal is pointing to his family land which is now on the other side of the Separation Wall from Abu Dis. His family lost three donums of land in the area of Khalit Abed and their family land was divided in two by Israel at the time that the Wall was built, so they lost the land and some of their olive trees. They can see the trees across the Wall, but they can't reach them.

Jamal explains that it is really terrible. The land was very important to them. About three years before the Wall was built, someone asked to buy the land and they refused because they love the land. It was a big shock for Jamal's father to see his land just taken away to make the Wall. He died a year ago. Before he died, his father told Jamal to take him to the land. So his sons took him, and they could see the land across the Wall. But it wasn't possible for the family to cross the Wall, so his father died without being able to go to his land. Not being able to go to the land at that time was very distressing for all of them.

Jamal Mohsen

JAMAL MOHSEN + ELIAS AYYAD, 2008

Elias shows the land that his father lost: one donum of land with ten olive trees, taken by Israel when the Separation Wall was built. His family depended on the olives from those trees. Up to four years ago they used to go there and take care of this land and collect the olives in the harvest season.

Losing the land to the Wall has been devastating. The first year after the Israelis finished the Wall, they gave the family a permit to go and collect the olives. That year the Civil Department made an announcement that people could come and apply for permits – not everybody, just old people and children – but in the years that followed this has not happened.

Since then they have not been able to go there. He wants to know who collects the olives each year, his family want to know but they haven't been able to find out.

Elias Ayyad

**Above: an Israeli military officer presenting
a land confiscation order to Abu Dis and
Sawahreh landowners in October 2007**

**Below right: the Israeli Separation Wall,
dividing Abu Dis houses (left) from their
olive groves in the valley**

New land confiscations

REPORTS FROM ABU DIS 2007–8

EXCERPT FROM ABU DIS HUMAN RIGHTS REPORT [1], OCTOBER 2007

In October 2007, more land was taken from Abu Dis for Israeli settlements and settlement roads.

On Tuesday 2nd October, the Israeli Minister of Homeland Security Avi Dikhtar announced that, at the beginning of the new year, the Israeli police commander of Judea and Samaria [2] would move to a new building based on the lands of Abu Dis and Azariyeh and that the police would start their official work in that building [3]. This did not take into account the United States' objections to the "E1 project"[4] because it would break the contiguity of the West Bank and would surround East Jerusalem with Jewish settlements, and end any opportunity for East Jerusalem to be the capital of a Palestinian state in the future.

On Thursday 11th October, the Israeli authorities announced military order T/19/07 to confiscate 1,100

donums (275 hectares) from the lands of Abu Dis and East Sawahreh, giving the pretext of opening a road for Palestinians between Bethlehem and Jericho. This decision was actually part of Israel's E1 project. They claim that this road shows that the E1 project will not affect the life of the Palestinians. But what they are doing is to build separate roads for Israeli settlers and for Palestinians and to cut Jerusalem completely from the Palestinians. Ghadi Shmenik the military commander of the Central Area of the West Bank [5] signed a decision on 24th September to take this land from Abu Dis, Sawahreh and Nabi Mousa.

On Wednesday 17th October, the Israelis gave another military order, T/35/07, to confiscate 386 donums and 300 sq metres from the lands of Azariyeh, Al-Tour (Mount of Olives) and Abu Dis …

On Thursday 18th October, the Israeli Mayor of the Jerusalem, Uri Lupolianski, announced that they were going to tender for the construction of 200,000 new Israeli settlement housing units in the different Arab neighbourhoods in East Jerusalem. The Israeli newspaper *Ha'aretz* mentioned that the Israeli local organising and building committee in Jerusalem decided last month to increase the number of settlers in Haret al-Yemen, in the middle of Silwan. This is with the full agreement of the Israeli government which is seeking to create facts on the ground before the Annapolis conference and the negotiations with the Palestinian side.

FOOTNOTES

[1] CADFA monthly human rights reports are on the website www.camdenabudis.net/

[2] The Israelis use the names of ancient kingdoms, Judea and Samaria, for the area of Palestine known to the world since 1948 as the West Bank.

[3] This new police station is built on agricultural land on its own, at a distance from the settlement of Maale Adumim; the local Palestinians have been expecting settlement building to expand to surround it since it was built. Therefore they knew it was part of the E1 project.

[4] The E1 project is a contentious project to settle huge areas of the middle of the West Bank, surrounding Jerusalem with settlements, joining Har Homa near Bethlehem, to Maale Adumim, east of Abu Dis and Pisgat Zeev near Hezma. It has been discussed internationally and twice the United States have said that they would not support Israel in pursuing the project. However it is clear that it is still an Israeli plan. See maps.

[5] There are separate Israeli military commanders for the north, middle and south of the West Bank.

Maale Adumim settlement built on Abu Dis land

Report from Cllr Bassam Bahar

The Bedouin village

The Israelis have recently been putting pressure on West Bank Bedouin, trying to bring them to live in a new village which they have been building for them on Abu Dis land. They are being pressured off land that they owned in other places. The plan is bad for the Bedouin who used to travel with their animals in a wide area, and living in a fixed place isn't acceptable to them. So far only 3,000 Bedouin have moved into the area (nowhere near the number Israel want), living in a new village that was created by the Israelis on Abu Dis land.

This plan is bad too for Abu Dis as this land has been taken away from families who wanted the land, and as they are losing a lot of land and being encircled by the Wall, it is hard to have a huge increase in population. Israel's plan is to have 25,000 Bedouin in that area, while the population of Abu Dis is somewhere around 10,000.

Bassam Bahar is a lawyer and local council member who is responsible for following the cases of the Wall and the land in Abu Dis

Bassam and other local lawyers have been working with some Bedouin families on this issue. In the area of Anata, the Israeli authority destroyed all the houses of a Bedouin family called Abu Dahouk. The local lawyers have been trying to find them an Israeli lawyer to bring a case in the Israeli court against the military decisions. They are also explaining to the Bedouin that the land they are moving to belongs to people in Abu Dis who care about their land - Israel is representing it as empty land with no owner but that isn't the case.

The Wall on the east side of Maale Adumim

The Israelis are planning to extend the settlements massively across the West Bank and around Jerusalem, and for that reason they are taking more land and building new sections of the Wall to cut off the Palestinian communities. They want to build a Wall on the east of Maale Adumim, five kilometres away from the settlement, taking many donums of land owned by Abu Dis families.

The council lawyer has been to court about this. He told the Israeli judge that Israel is talking about the

security of the settlement and that if that is the reason
for the Wall, it is meant for security, it would be put
it round the settlement, not five kilometres from it,
which means that Abu Dis people will lose around 30
square kilometres of land.

The judge told him that this issue is dealt with by the
Israeli Ministry of Defence and until they have made a
decision, the courts cannot deal with it.

Below: Palestinian olive grove, Abu Dis

**Below right: Abu Dis land taken to become
rubbish dump for Israeli settlement**

Rubbish dump and fears of cancer

In 1986, the Israeli authorities gave a piece of land – ten donums– that belonged to the Badr family of Abu Dis – to the Israeli municipality in Jerusalem to use as a rubbish dump for the whole of Jerusalem. This land was agricultural land before that, and was being used by the Badr family and their neighbours.

Of course when the Israelis wanted ten donums, they didn't just take ten, but they took over all the land around it and declared that it was a closed military area and that nobody was allowed to reach it. As a result, in the past twenty years, the Israelis have extended the area of the rubbish tip to fifty donums. It is now very close to the houses in Abu Dis and specially to the new village that the Israelis built for the Bedoin.

The effects of this area are not just on the environment in general, but it affects human beings badly. In the area of East Jerusalem, round Abu Dis, there is the highest incidence of cancer in the West Bank, and I think that this is because people are living close to the rubbish dump on the east side of Abu Dis.

In the past three years, the Israelis have started to

BASSAM BAHAR, 2008

bring some sort of black liquid (maybe effluent from industries?) and put it in big pools they have built in the valley between Sawahreh and Abu Dis. They bring it in special cars from somewhere inside Israel, and sometimes they come and take it back again. Local people don't know what it is. B'tselem has done some research and is suggesting that there is some sort of radiation in the three square kilometres around the area.[1]

There are signs saying that the liquid is poison and that people should not come close. But it is very close to the houses, specially to the Bedouin whom Israel have resettled on that land, and worryingly there are often children playing in the around it. The Israelis appear to be building more pools both to the east and the west.

Abu Dis local council was started in 1996 [1]. Since then we have been trying to make a good system for the rubbish from Abu Dis. The Israeli authorities refuse to allow Abu Dis rubbish to go in that area, unless we pay 4,500 shekels a month. This is an impossible sum for Abu Dis council but we don't have anywhere else for it to go. Abu Dis council can sometimes afford it and sometimes we can't, which means that the rubbish remains in the streets of Abu Dis.

Local Palestinians don't have land to organise landfill themselves so other councils also put their rubbish there if they can afford to – the Bethlehem area, for example.

In 2000, the Israeli municipality of Jerusalem gave this area to a private Israeli company, which now works on the lands around in any way they want. It started with Badr family land, and now they have taken Ayyad family land and land belonging to the Eriqat and Abu Fseissiyeh families as well. Abu Dis local council recently went to the Israeli military authority to ask them not to use any extra land but they haven't had a satisfactory answer.

When the Israelis planned the Wall on the east side of Abu Dis, they decided that this area would be on the Abu Dis side not on the settlement side, but they will still bring rubbish there.

FOOTNOTE

[1] See photo on page 34.

The environment around Abu Dis

In 40 years of occupation and control by Israel over Jerusalem and its suburbs, Israel hasn't had any interest in the health of the people under occupation. The people in the east of Jerusalem have not been allowed to make a sewage-processing plant, and Israel builds its rubbish tips right by the towns and causes many environmental problems for people in the West Bank by taking away lands and cutting trees on them and making settlement roads and building the Wall ... All of this has made life in this area very hard.

They want the land for something different

Their view of what to use the land for is different from ours. They want to bring more and more settlers from all over the world to place them on our land. They are scarring the land everywhere. They are

ABDUL WAHAB SABBAH, 2008

making hundreds of new roads and the Wall. They are building settlements (new towns) and military areas everywhere.

Hardly any of them want to use the land for agriculture whereas the basic thing the Palestinians want to do is use the land to grow things The Israelis are doing all they can to drive the Palestinians away from their land. We have a strong relationship to the land, we want to grow things on it. For us the land means life.

It is a basic part of their policy to upset Palestinian agriculture. They take over the land, they cut down the trees. It is because they want the Palestinians to leave.

Caring for the environment?

Israel presents itself as caring for the environment, but the point is that building settlements on the West Bank is the opposite of caring for the environment. They said that Jabal Abu Ghnaim was a nature reserve and then they built thousands of settlement

The sign says: "Entry forbidden. Danger of drowning! Poisonous material!"

housing units on it. They use the West Bank like a rubbish tip for them and they are taking over most of our water.

The electric wires on the Separation Wall are killing birds and the Wall stops animals migrating (as well as people travelling).

Palestinians have been prevented from walking in the hills to gather herbs that they used to (sage, thyme). The Israelis brought dogs from Israel that can be dangerous and set them free in the hills. In Abu Dis you can hear them barking every night.

Sewage river

If you go to the area between Sawahreh and Bethlehem you see a river. Visitors from Europe think it is a river. In fact it's the sewage from settlements in West Jerusalem and East Jerusalem and it flows through Palestinian land and it spoils the agriculture. It goes right to the Dead Sea. The Israelis also take all sorts of minerals from the Dead Sea.

Water

The Dead Sea is half the size it was in 1967 because the Israelis drain the water from the River Jordan which flows into the Dead Sea. Actually they diverted a large part of the river and they drained the Howla Lake that used to be near Beesan. It is a big problem for the Palestinians that the water is taken from the River Jordan. People need it and so do the agricultural lands.

The Israelis have also taken control of the main aquifers in the West Bank – they have built settlements to control them. The Israelis have made different regulations for the Palestinians and the Israeli settlers with regard to water extraction.

So it has become difficult and expensive for the Palestinians to get water themselves and they are dependent on the Israeli water company to supply water. So they control the water pressure and the quantity and quality of water that comes to Abu Dis.

In Abu Dis, the Water Society does an annual maintenance of the water pipes to ensure that the water supply is clean. The Israelis don't let them do this now for the water pipes in the area on the west of the Wall, and so some people are now using water filters to ensure that the water that they drink is clean.

Left: The poisonous black liquid in Israel's pool on Abu Dis land

Below: Jabal Abu Ghnaim, near Bethlehem, was taken by Israel for a nature reserve – and then they built the settlement of Har Homa on it

Al Quds between the past and the present, and the promised future

SIRAT SANDOUQA, 2008

Sirat Sandouqa, a headteacher in Abu Dis, comes from the old city of Jerusalem. That was ten minutes from Abu Dis before the Wall was built. Now it is a long journey through uncertain checkpoints: travelling miles round to enter Abu Dis from the opposite side

Who does not love Jerusalem and who does not find peace, tranquillity and intoxication when he sees the Dome of the Rock from outside the walls of the old city, or when he passes through its gates and walks in its narrow streets and alleys. Its sons cried when they departed from it.

Jerusalem is a historic city, full of cultural heritage, archaeological remains and the visual evidence of the importance of this city. It is the mirror that reflects the depth of the Arabic Islamic presence. There are ancient buildings that were built for specific purposes of the time, such as small chapels, and religious charitable foundations, places to tie horses, drinking fountains, public baths, graveyards, inns and other things besides. And there are still old houses, old places built for animals and shops for selling and buying things.

And this is a holy religious place. In the beginning of Islam people used to pray towards Jerusalem, and it has the third most holy mosque. Also it has the Church of the Holy Sepulchre and so it is a holy city for millions of followers of different religions.

It is the pulse of the Palestinian heart and the umbilicus of the nation: Jerusalem is the centre for Palestinian people and its address.

And it includes the biggest and the most important institutions. Also the city is a market and it has international economic significance as far as tourism is concerned, and many people have poured into to the city because everything in it is beautiful and attractive.

When you enter Damascus Gate, which is the main gate for the Holy City, you come on to its market of street sellers with small barrows, money-changers, women villagers who sell vegetables and produce of the generous Palestinian land: the white cucumbers of the countryside, dbouki grapes from Hebron and Khader, the fresh thyme and sage of the Palestinian hills. And there are coffee shops, Siam Cafe, Zaatara Cafe, the place where people from the city and the countryside have met.

It is deeply sad that the people from around Jerusalem and outside it can't enter the Holy City any more. Because the Israeli authorities have annexed it, and built the wall of isolation and expansion, and the city has become cut off from its suburbs and from the rest of the West Bank. And the Israelis built a museum under Damascus Gate market.

In the past, and during Ramadan evenings, you could find storytellers in Mona Café near Al Wadi Road, which comes to Damascus Gate market. The story teller was Abu Saleh whose lovely stories I remember. When you go forward along Al Wadi Road, you could find Al Hospice Café and Al Kassas Café and other ones. Most of these cafes don't exist any more, and the Israelis took over the whole of Al Wadi Road to build18 clusters of settlements and a synagogue. They started to dig tunnels connecting Al Wadi road and Al Buraq square in the Moroccan quarter and as a result of that, forty-nine Palestinian families were forced out of their houses and left the area.

As you go along the Al Wadi Road towards the Al Aqsa mosque, the area is full of Palestinian families who are refugees from 1948. And a road used by Jews leads to Al Buraq Square [1].

As for the markets of the old city, there is Bab Khan al-Zeit market which is the longest and most crowded in the old city. It was called this name [2] because it includes the places to sell olive oil and olives, in the season. You can find there all you wish of popular restaurants including the famous Zalatimo and Ja'afar sweetshops. You used to find there hand-made goods which are no longer available, and the people who could fix primus stoves, solder tanks or make rubber buckets.

The Israeli settlers have managed, with the help of the Jewish state, to create two settlements inside the main market by taking over the places called Hawsh al-Sherwish and Aqabat al-Takiya.

At the end of Bab Khan al-Zeit market you can go directly to Al Dabaghah market (leather market) Al Lahamin market (blacksmiths' market) and the market

of the perfume-sellers.

In the Al Dabaghah market is the Church of the Holy Sepulchre, which used to be very crowded with tourists from different nationalities and religions. Unfortunately now you can't see many of them there. Also exactly in the middle of this market you used to see a pond with fountains, and around it the Afghans with their traditional dress, who used to sharpen knives. This also doesn't exist any more now because the settlers from Atarot Kohenim took over a big building which is called Pension Mar Yohanna, next to the Holy Sepulchre Church.

To the west of Al Dabaghah market is the market of the Christian quarter, leading to Khanaka road which joins to Khan al-Zeit and has small shops for souvenirs, china, candles, olive-wood models and goods made of shell.

One of the industries that used to be very famous was the Aqrouq Brothers factory for Turkish hats [3]. Now the market is very weak and the Atarot Kohenim have taken control of part of the area of the Christian quarter.

And from the Al Dabaghah market to the three other markets, blacksmiths and perfume and the Souq al-Khawajat (foreigners' market) - which used to be called al-Sagha in the past - where people worked with gold. And all of it famous for different kinds of meat, vegetables, perfume, cloth and other things.

And it was full of people selling and buying. In one place you could see the copper market, where tinkers used to clean and polish copper utensils. You used to see them rubbing the utensils with their feet, swaying their hips from side to side, and the pots would be shiny again in no time.

But these markets are not safe at the moment, because there are settlers on the roofs, specially on the building which is called Dar al-Sabra, which they call Glytzia School. The small market of the Bab al-Silsila which stretched from the gate of the Al Aqsa Mosque to the Bab al-Khalil included Al Beezar market and the small Al Loon market. Now nothing remains of these markets except one sesame press, because the settlers took over properties and shops

in Bab al-Silsila in the south and also took over two hotels and some of the shops in Omar Ibn al-Khatab Square and Bab al-Khalil area.

The south area of the old city of Jerusalem turned into a Jewish neighbourhood after the Israeli authority took over the whole of the Moroccan quarter and other areas.

Once upon a time the markets of Jerusalem were choking with people, especially on the Muslim and Christian holidays, and on the days of Al Nabi Mousa season [4].

When you go outside the walls of the old city, to the street of Sultan Suleiman, or to Salah al-Din Street or Sheikh Jarrah, all these streets hold the names of great Muslim leaders.

The west side of the city was occupied in 1948, and was turned into a Jewish area. In 1967 the Zionists took control of the rest of the holy city. East Jerusalem is altogether 70.5 km sq. Israel put 24 km

sq, which is thirty-three percent of the east side of the city, under the direct control of Israel. It built fifteen Jewish settlement areas, which brought in a huge Jewish population of 185,000 settlers, where there were none in 1967.

Forty percent of East Jerusalem was put under the indirect authority of the Israelis through confiscating lands supposedly for public use, through its "skeleton map" [5], through building new roads and declaring nature reserves.

Israel took control of properties and land inside the Arab neighbourhoods like Sheikh Jarrah, Silwan, Ras al-Amoud and Jabal al-Zeitun (Mount of Olives); and to make it easy for the Zionist movement to Judaise Jerusalem, they built the Separation Wall, which, around the city, is 88 km. This wall changed this city from a central city into a border city, bringing very bad circumstances in all spheres of life – economic, educational, social, health and all other things.

So, Rose of Cities and Jewel of Palestine, your streets no longer tell the generations of Jerusalem the stories of their fathers and grandfathers. But what goes on in the minds and souls of the people of this nation, the expression of their suffering, and the sacrifices that individuals and groups offer, all show that the body of this nation is still alive and full of energy, waiting to be employed in the right direction.

FOOTNOTES

[1] This has now been made into the Wailing Wall Plaza

[2] Zeit is oil

[3] In Arabic, tarboush; in Britain they are known as fez

[4] In April, people used to walk out of Jerusalem on a pilgrimage to Nabi Mousa. Now the Separation Wall is in the way

[5] A plan for the Judaisation of the city of Jerusalem

Life in Abu Dis

In the past without checkpoints life was easier. Anybody who wanted to work and anybody who wanted to go to hospital or to school or to a party in a hotel or on a journey or shopping could go to markets and pray in Al Aqsa Mosque and we could get to Bethlehem or to Haifa or Jaffa or Hebron – any place in Palestine.

But now we are feeling miserable because everything is closed to us, and every city or village is like a prison. We can't go to any place or any city or village in the West Bank. We are feeling sad, very sad, from this cause. We are feeling like dead without Jerusalem.

The soldiers do not give permits to anybody who wants to go to any place. They tell us "Go to your home; if you don't go I will kill you." The men soldiers are very disrespectful to women and girls.

The Occupation soldiers are kind of terrorists.

In the end we have this Wall, separating families. For example, I have three sisters in the other part behind the Wall. This means I have not seen them for more than two years. This condition seems like South Africa, but it is worse, because all our life is imprisoned by this Wall – our school, our hospitals, our university, and Al-Aqsa Mosque. For example if a pregnant woman wants to go to hospital, the soldier may not let her, so one woman had her baby born at the checkpoint. Another bad case is if any student has an exam, sometimes he cannot go because the soldiers stop and sometimes arrest him, so he misses the exam.

Also we don't have any garden or places to go for fun, so as a result our life is unhappy for ourselves and our children and all Palestinian people. So we need this Occupation to end.

REDA JAFFAL, APRIL 2006

Forbidden to have a baby

REPORT FROM ABU DIS, APRIL 07

Rasha's baby, Mohammed Aamer

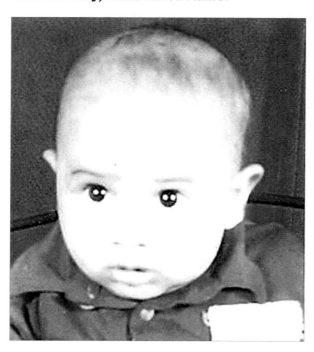

On Sunday 29th April 07, early in the morning, Rasha Abu al-Rish was in labour. She went at 1am with her husband to Al Bawabeh checkpoint to go to Jerusalem, trying to reach the hospital to have her baby. The soldiers refused to allow them to pass through the checkpoint.

So they went to the big Al Zeituneh terminal. Her husband called his mother-in-law to come and help explain to the soldiers. After 45 minutes arguing with the soldiers, they still refused to let them through. Rasha was in pain, her husband was very upset and angry, but the soldiers didn't want to listen.

Then her husband had the idea of calling one of his friends from Jerusalem – he woke him at 2 in the morning and asked him to come to collect Rasha. The friend agreed. He had to drive east towards Maale Adumim settlement and come to Abu Dis, a long way round. Then he took Rasha and returned back the same way, driving east before he could turn west to Jerusalem.

They had to leave her husband as there was no way they could take him in the car, but even taking Rasha, with her green pass, was a risk for the driver, as according to Israeli rules, Rasha wasn't allowed to be in that car.

They went back to Jerusalem through a third checkpoint, and this time Rasha (now really uncomfortable) was lucky – the soldiers did not ask for her ID – and she managed to reach the hospital alone, leaving her husband on the other side of the Wall.

Inside the hospital there is no service for mobile phones. Rasha was lucky that she knew one of the doctors who was able to ring her husband when the baby was born. Three days later she travelled back to Abu Dis with the baby, along with some women with Jerusalem IDs.

Born at a checkpoint

REPORT FROM ABU DIS, MARCH 07

On Sunday, 13th March 2007, Afaf Bader from Abu Dis went to the Civil Department together with her husband to get a permit to go to Jerusalem. She had with her a letter from Al Maqassed Hospital saying that she had to go to the delivery room in the hospital to give birth. But at the Civil Department they asked her to wait and wait until at the end she had her baby Shahendah at the checkpoint.

Afaf Baher and baby Shahendah

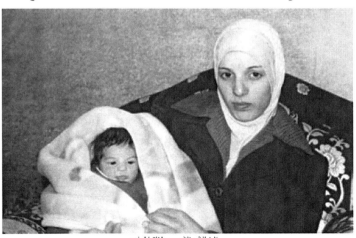

بعد منعها من الوصول الى المستشفى من خلال معبر الزيتون

المواطنة عفاف بحر تضع مولودتها شهندة على مرأى ومسمع الجيش الاسرائيلي

المواطنة عفاف بحر وطفلتها شهندة

My grandmother

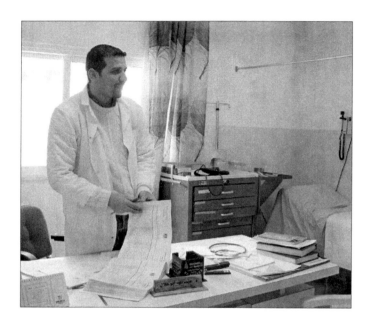

Today at 2 o'clock this morning, my grandmother (80 years old) started to have acute and severe rectal bleeding. We called the ambulance to take her to the Al Maqassed hospital in Jerusalem. It was a Palestinian ambulance, and the driver said that the soldiers at the checkpoint would not allow our ambulance to go through to Jerusalem, and he advised us to call an Israeli ambulance.

We called the Israeli one, and they asked for the number of my grandmother's ID, and mine as well, and asked us to call back after five minutes. After five minutes we called them and they said that she could go to the hospital, but I could not, because of the security of Israel, as I am not allowed to go to Jerusalem. I then gave them two other ID numbers to check if they were allowed (my sister and cousin), while my grandmother was still bleeding. After five minutes, I called them and they said that my sister and cousin could not go either, for the same reason.

Then we asked someone who has a blue ID to go with her. By the time she arrived at the hospital, she was in a very severe situation. Her Hb was 9 and they took her to the intensive care unit, where they had to give her three units of blood. They said that she needed more, but they did not have any more. The problem was that no one from her family in Abu Dis could go to Jerusalem to give blood, and none of her daughters or sons could go to stay with her.

She is still bleeding and her situation is still very bad, and because of the severity of the bleeding, the doctors cannot do anything.

We have called some people who have blue IDs to give her blood, but they are not the same blood group. We are trying to organize tomorrow, in our clinic in Abu Dis, a day with Al Maqassed hospital to take blood from the people who have the same blood group (I am one of them), and then send it to the hospital, if she is still alive.

DR ABDULLAH ABU HILAL, 2006

Blood transfusion

DR ABDULLAH ABU HILAL

Above: Al Hajeh Sabreah with her son at Muabar Al Zaytoneh, one of the huge checkpoints in the Separation Wall; and ...

Below: waiting in Al Muqassed Medical Centre in Abu Dis – first for permission from the Israeli side and then for a blood transfusion

On 14 April Al Hajeh Sabreah Abu Helal, 83 years old, came to the Al Maqassed medical clinic in the West Bank town of Abu Dis, complaining of general weakness and difficulty of breath. After many investigations she was discovered to have acute anaemia (her haemoglobin was 6). She was referred to Al Muqassed Hospital in Jerusalem to investigate the cause of the anaemia, and for a blood transfusion.

We, as usual, sent a special report to the hospital. This was then sent to the Israeli side in order to find out if she could obtain permission to enter Jerusalem. After a long wait we were informed that she couldn't be given a permit for security reasons. Her son went to the Mu'abar Al Zaytuneh and attempted to persuade soldiers there to allow his mother to pass through to the hospital, but the soldiers refused.

After several telephone calls to human rights organisations in Israel, she was given permission to go to the hospital alone, without anyone from her family, who have also been refused for security reasons.

At 4 o'clock in the afternoon, the ambulance was called and she was taken to the Al Zayem checkpoint to go to hospital. But after checking her ID and her son's ID, the soldiers at the checkpoint told them that her son should return home, and that she should go to the hospital by Israeli ambulance and pay 600 Israeli shekels.

Human rights organizations were called again until they agreed to let her go to the hospital with her son in the same ambulance.

She is now in hospital alone, and no one from her family can visit her.

Danger to the state?

Our dear friends in Camden:

We send the most beautiful of greetings from Abu Dis the steadfast.

The situation has become very bad. A few months from now, Abu Dis will become isolated and will become a prison.

What happened on Sunday 26th March 06 is the most striking example that the Israeli government has gone mad. On this day, a young woman contacted me, crying, around 9 in the evening, begging for help. "My husband Ayoub has lost consciousness and he is not breathing." Ayoub is a young man from Abu Dis – his full name is Ayoub Abu Hilal – and he is 26 years of age. He has a brother who suffers from heart disease and high blood pressure and who had a heart operation and a mother who is suffering from the same ailment in addition to diabetis. He also had a brother who died a year ago at the age of 45. This person, Ayoub, got married a year and a half ago. His wife is 18 years of age.

DR ABDULLAH ABU HILAL

Ayoub Abu Hilal

When I got to his house, everybody was crying and wailing. I found the ambulance people there, trying to give him first aid. When I examined him, I found him almost dead, but I couldn't tell his family that this was the case. I informed them that we had to take him to hospital immediately. We co-ordinated with the Israeli ambulance service to take them to hospital.

We put him in a Palestinian ambulance and left the area and continued attending to him in the ambulance, until we got to Maale Adumim settlement where an Israeli ambulance was waiting for us. An Israeli doctor present at the Israeli ambulance tried with us to revive him, but 20 minutes later it had become certain that he was dead, so we had to take him to the al-Muqassed hospital in East Jerusalem to keep him in the morgue until the morning so that they could bury him in Abu Dis the following morning.

But on the checkpoint, and despite the fact that the Israeli soldiers manning the checkpoint knew that he was dead, and despite the Israeli doctor's report that we should take him to the morgue, the Israeli soldiers refused under the pretext that the checkpoint was shut for security reasons, and that no one without an Israeli identity card could go to Jerusalem, even if he was dead.

So we started thinking what we should do with this body. Should we take him home to his family so that they would be even more devastated, especially as they were expecting him to come back with us, smiling as he usually did when he was alive. So we decided to save them the tragedy. We decided that I and one of his relatives should go back to tell them the bad news, while the ambulance crew would take him to the anatomy department in the Al-Quds University in Abu Dis.

I don't want to tell you about the rest of the story – It was a very painful tragedy when his mum and his wife and the rest of the family knew about the death.

The University agreed to keep his body in their fridge after contacting lots of people. So we buried him this morning. And we are asking the question – does a dead person constitute a danger to their state?

Killed at the checkpoint

REPORT FROM ABU DIS , MAY 2006

Shehadah Mohsen tried very hard to get to his hospital appointment. He had to try three checkpoints as he was repeatedly prevented by soldiers from going to Jerusalem. He first went to the Bawabeh checkpoint in Abu Dis, then went to Al-Zeitunah terminal – he was prevented from passing at both of them. So he went to Sawahreh, south of Abu Dis, to the Sheikh Saad checkpoint

Abu Dis has a shahid today [1]

Today, 23/05/2006, Mr Shehadah Ahmad Mohsen, 52 years old, wanted to go to Al Maqassed Hospital in Jerusalem for his regular Tuesday follow-up appointment in connection with his diabetis, hypertension and ischemic heart disease.

All the ways and gates were closed. He tried to go through Sheikh Saad checkpoint [2], but the soldiers who were there stopped him and started to hit him with their guns on his head. He started to bleed and then he died.

Shehadah Mohsen was a poor man. He has sons and daughters. His only fault was that he wanted to have medical treatment in his hospital which is in his city Jerusalem.

FOOTNOTES

[1] Shahid (martyr) is the word Palestinians use for
     people who have been killed by the Israeli military.

Sheikh Saad checkpoint

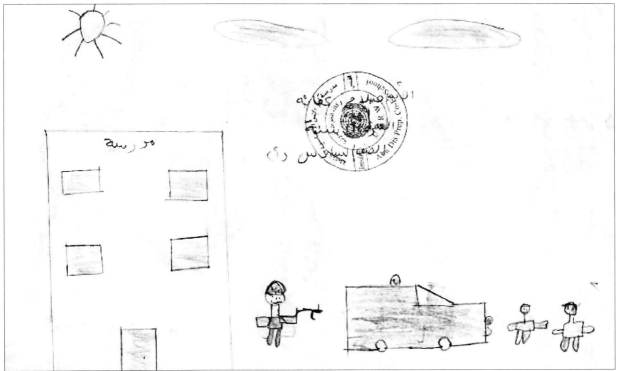

I want my childhood back

One day I woke up very frightened to the horrible sound of military vehicles next to my house. I hurried to the window to see what was happening. I saw something that caused me so much pain. I saw these huge vehicles and bulldozers uprooting the trees of the small church near our house.

I was pained. Every tree that was pulled out resembled an organ of my body, it was as if my organs were being pulled out. I shouted and the whole house shook. So my mother woke up frightened and she said "What's wrong with you, my daughter?"

I said to her "Look, there, look, they are uprooting the trees that we used to play under". We used to go there and the priest used to meet us. I used to hang my swing on one of the trees and relax. Now it is gone.

Everything caused my father to stop his work so things are different from before. My father doesn't bring me clothes or food. He quarrels with my mum every day. He says to her "I need to work. I need some money to feed my children". When I ask him to bring me something from the shop, he says the shopkeeper doesn't want to sell us anything.

We sold everything in our house and nothing is left. This is my childhood. It has gone; it has been destroyed. Ach, ach and a thousand achs.

Why is it that every child in the world can enjoy their childhood while mine has been destroyed? I would like to repeat :

I want my childhood back.
I want my childhood back.
I want my childhood back.

RANA SAMIH GHABBASH, AGE 13
2005

The separating apartheid Wall

OMAR ARAR, AGED 12
2005

My name is Omar. I am a Palestinian child. I was born in Jerusalem the holy city. My mother told me that people were free to move in all the country in those days. Palestine was one park. Although we are living in some Jerusalem suburb which is called the West Bank, my mother used to go shopping from Ramallah, Bethlehem whenever she wanted and she used to visit different places in Jerusalem and we used to move freely for treatment, for teaching. Travel from Jerusalem to Ramallah takes 20 minutes.

When I was born, my father was an actor. He had many friends and he used to take us to many places to visit his friends. But they were poor. My mother said that I got sick in those days in Jerusalem. Our home was small and cold but we were lucky because there was not shooting there or missiles, unlike what happened in the West Bank.

After the Wall our country became like a prison, our parents are not working and their presence in Jerusalem is considered a crime. Now I can't go to swim. I can't go to see the museum, or to the theatre. Now there are 700 checkpoints in Palestine and when we look at the Wall, it looks very terrifying.

The Wall hides the Al Aqsa from our eyes but not from our hearts. After the Wall, life changed. Many people left the country. Many businesses closed and until now they are going on building the Wall and they are bringing more strangers to our country who are living in our country and moving freely for their work, for their schools.

Now with all these troubles, our love for Palestine will not be less. The old people tell the new generation how it was a good life in this country. There are photos, there are movies and there are memories and they are not finished.

Voices from Abu Dis Boys' School

This is us, walking in Abu Dis.

صورتنا ونحن نتجول في شوارع ابوديس

This is Abu Dis.

This picture is of the separation wall.

It is very long!

صورة للجدار الفاصل الضخم في

ابوديس الجدار طويل جداً

The wall is very big.

It stops us from going to Jerusalem.

We have family we can't see.

We wish we could push it over!

الجدار ضخم جداً ويمنعنا من الذهاب الى

القدس لدينا اهل واقارب هناك لا نستطيع رؤيتهم!

نتمنى ان نسقط الجدار

This is a picture of the wall.

Our land is getting smaller.

صورة للجدار ارضنا اصبحت اصغر

THESE BOYS FROM ABU DIS SCHOOL
TOOK PHOTOS OF ABU DIS
AND WROTE IN ENGLISH TO EXPLAIN THEM:

ANAS ABU FARAH
ESHAQ ESHAQ
ABDULRAHMAN ABED RABO
DARWESH KHANAFESEH
ATA MOUSA HALABEH

2008

The Container checkpoint

The Container checkpoint is on the road south of Abu Dis that leads to Bethlehem.

My house in Sawahreh is above the Container checkpoint. Every day in the morning and the evening I see the queues of traffic there. The Israeli soldiers don't let the cars pass through, but they are not checking the cars. They check some IDs. They don't really care about that. Mainly they block the way and hold up people on their way to work and back. Often they just go into the room they have there and turn on music and put their feet up and listen to it, and outside the queue grows and grows and people get later and later. They often keep the road shut for an hour or so in the middle of the rush hour. They just want to make people nervous and angry.

The checkpoints on Palestinian land are not for any real thing. They are not looking for anything, but they want to make Palestinian life impossible.

Quite a lot of people here have blue (Jerusalem) IDs, like I do. The Israelis won't let people with blue IDs

SARAH SALAMEH, 2008

through the checkpoint to Bethlehem at all. Last week my mother-in-law was ill and we needed to take her to the hospital in Beit Jala [1]. Because I have a blue ID, they wouldn't let me go through the checkpoint with her. If I go to Bethlehem I have to go another way, over the hills.

The main market for animals is in Bethelehem, so farmers have to bring their animals in trucks along the road and through the checkpoint. But they are forbidden to bring their animals through, so the farmers have to take the animals out of the trucks and walk them down the hill and round the checkpoint and then bring the truck through and load them up again.

School students here whose parents have blue IDs go to school in Jerusalem. They have to go through the Shayyah checkpoint. They get there at six in the morning to try and get past the queue by 7.30 so they can get the school bus on the other side of the checkpoint. The soldiers give them a hard time. They look through their bags, they make them take

off their jackets and take off their shoes. Often they just don't open the checkpoint until a huge crowd of students are there, or they wait till the school buses have gone and then they open the checkpoint and the students have to go through the checkpoint and then they have to walk to school. When they come back and they are not in a hurry, the soldiers let them through quickly, no problem.

FOOTNOTE

[1] Next to Bethlehem

Getting a permit for my grandfather

A LETTER FROM A CHILD IN ABU DIS TO CADFA

There is a new suffering that the Israeli forces are making the people in the towns of Abu Dis, Azariyeh and Sawahreh endure.

It was a month ago that the Israeli forces build a terminal that they called Al Zeitunah which separates Aizariyeh and Jerusalem. This terminal is the only way to Jerusalem. It isn't possible to go through it unless you have a special permit and that is only given to ill people or people who work there.

Today I suffered a big problem because I went there to get a permit for my grandfather, because he had to have open heart surgery and treatment in hospital and he needs a permit so he can stay in the hospital. So for this reason I was there from 8 in the morning until 3 in the afternoon, and I waited until they gave me a permit.

This is a very big problem and we are suffering a lot from it because the terminal prevents people getting to Jerusalem and prevents ill people from getting to their hospitals for treatment. I really hope for some help from you all with this.

MOHAMMED IBRAHIM ABU HILAL
OCTOBER 2006

Greetings to our friends in Camden.

Blue and green IDs

The Israelis give West Bankers green ID cards (some older people still have orange ones), and Palestinian residents of Jerusalem blue ID cards.

My name is Fatheah Abu Hilal, and I am from Beit Hanina, a town near Jerusalem. I have five brothers and five sisters, and I am the oldest child in our family. I want to tell you that Beit Hanina is divided into pieces by the Apartheid Wall. My father has a green (West Bank) ID and my mother has the blue (Jerusalem) ID. When I was born, my mother was 13 years old and did not then have any ID. So my parents put me on my father's ID. When my mother was sixteen she was given a blue ID, and so all my brothers and sisters were put her blue ID.

When I was sixteen years old I was given, like my father, a green ID. I then married in Abu Dis and my husband also has a green ID. After this my mother managed to get my father a blue ID. So because I am married to a West Banker, I am the only person in my family with a green ID.

Before the Wall, it was easier to pass through to the other side of Beit Hanina. There used to be areas of the barrier which were low enough to climb over. But now the Wall is nine meters high and completely closed, so this is now impossible .

If I want to go to visit my family I must obtain a permit. The only way to get this is for medical reasons. Sometimes I go to the hospital and pay for a check-up that I don't really need, to get to the other side of the Wall, and I must get a piece of paper to prove I have been, because if I don't do this, the hospital will not give me permission to go another time.

One time, Israeli soldiers stopped me in the street near my family home in Beit Hanina. On this day I had managed to climb over the barrier (before the wall was completed) to visit my family. They asked what I was doing there with a green ID, and said that I was not allowed to be there. They took me away and made me wait for three hours. Then they interrogated me. I told them that this was my city and I was born, raised and educated here, and that I had just come to visit my family.

FATHEAH ABU HILAL, NOVEMBER 2006

They took my fingerprints and put my details on record, and because of that it is now more difficult for me to go to Beit Hanina. I must wait for my family to come to visit me here in Abu Dis. It is not easy for them to come and visit me so I don't see them very often. They come for Eid just for 10 minutes or so as they have so many other people to visit. If my family wants to visit me they must go a long way round as the Wall is in the way.

There are times when it is very important to go to your home town, for example weddings and funerals. However I am not able to go to these.

I also know so many families in the same or similar situations, some husbands and wives can't live together if they have different colour IDs. This is one of my problems.

The Wall in Abu Dis separates many families, husbands and wives, parents and children. I have a friend, her name is Sohad, she lives in Sheyyah, and her husband lives in Abu Dis. She has five children. There is a gate nearby. Her husband called her one day and asked her to come quickly as there were no soldiers near the gate. When he started to climb the gate, the soldiers came. So the father had to jump back the way he came. The mother came with her child who started to cry when they saw their father. She asked, "Why are you crying?" Her child said, "I want to see my father!" She said, "You saw him! He tried to jump but he couldn't."
But the child said "No! I saw his jacket, not his face!"

Blue and green IDs

Separating families

MOIEN ALEMOUR, 2008

My name is Moien Alemour. I was born in 1969 in Rummaneh, a village 12 km away from Jenin. In 1998, I moved to Abu Dis which is 2km from Jerusalem, to work at the Arab Institute as an English teacher.

In 2001 I got married to a girl who holds a Jerusalem ID card. At that time it didn't seem to be a problem for either of us. Between 2001 and 2008, we had four children, three daughters and a son. Only two months after she was born, our eldest daughter Malakah died.

Palestinian access to East Jerusalem was tightened in September 2000 with the outbreak of the Second Intifada. A series of additional military checkpoints and obstacles were set up to further restrict Palestinian movement into Jerusalem, Israel and also within the West Bank itself. In 2001 the Israeli government announced its intention to build a barrier to physically separate Israel from the West Bank.

As a Jerusalem ID holder and to maintain her card under Israeli law and to register our three children on her ID card, my wife has to show that Jerusalem is her centre of life and that she lives inside the Jerusalem boundaries. So she is forced to provide a proof that she lives in a house in Jerusalem to ensure that she retains her Jerusalem status because the law continues to force Palestinian residents of Jerusalem to make hard choices about where to establish their lives.

But unlike my wife, I hold a West Bank ID card and to obtain a permit to live inside Jerusalem is not something easy. So we both face extreme difficulties in having a clear vision for the future. The Israeli Interior Ministry will not permit the registration of our children unless we prove our permanent Jerusalem residence.

No-one is blamed in this situation, neither me nor my wife, because everyone explains and sees things according to their own point of view and each one of us is right when a decision arises. For example, West Bank ID card holders who want to travel even within the West Bank itself suffer a lot from many different things: time-consuming humiliation, waiting for long hours, crossing more than one checkpoint, walking a long distance… To avoid her children suffering, my wife is doing her very best to register our children on her Jerusalem ID card. As for me, I am paying too much money for this issue and I cannot any longer bear the cost of lawyers' fees and the arnona (Jerusalem taxes) and other things. So it is an additional burden I face which makes life more difficult, expensive and even disgusting.

After a long time of suffering I was a little bit fortunate to find a small house outside the Wall which is still considered like the houses inside the Jerusalem boundaries. But here also another problem arises. When I applied to obtain a permit to enter Jerusalem, my application was rejected on the pretext that I don't need a permit because my work is in Abu Dis and we live outside the Wall. Also, knowing my need for this house, the owner of it always badly blackmails me, increasing the rent and threatening to kick me out unless I pay what he imposes.

Other funny things. Since my wife holds a Jerusalem ID card, and she has a driving licence, we have bought a car that has an Israeli plate. Once upon a time, when we were travelling to Jenin to visit my parents there, our car was stopped at an Israeli checkpoint and we were forced to show our ID cards. Really I was very surprised to hear the Israeli soldiers asking me to leave the car because as a West Bank ID-carrier I was not allowed to be in an Israeli car although I told him that I was with my family, my wife and my children, and I was in

Palestinian Authority territories. He insisted on me getting out of the car.

Another similar incident. While we were also travelling to Jenin with my wife and my children, after travelling more than 100 km, we were stopped by an Israeli checkpoint only 10 km from Jenin. As usual, we were asked to show our personal ID cards. An Israeli soldier shouted at us, saying "Don't you know that Jerusalem ID-card holders are prohibited from entering areas under Palestinian Authority control? You (and he meant me) are the only one who can continue travelling to Jenin, but your wife, children and the car must immediately go back now." That forced us to go back together to search for another way to get to Jenin.

So the barriers do not only physically separate Israelis from the West Bank or separate West Bank from Jerusalem or cut through the Palestinian community or divide the neighbourhoods or divide the city itself into two parts, but its security restrictions also extend to separating a father from his children and his wife inside their car in the West Bank.

From 2002 until now, we have been waiting to register our three children Malakah, Mustafa and Dania, and I have also been waiting to obtain a permit to enter Jerusalem, despite providing and performing all the legally required documents and stipulations. Now I think that I have the right to ask what more is needed?

Open Letter to the United Nations Secretary General

Dear Sir

I am a Palestinian citizen living in the town of Abu Dis in the eastern part of Jerusalem. I am married and the father of three children, the oldest being 5 years of age. As a father, I have the duty to provide and look after my family, and to protect them and live with them. I am sure that this is the duty of any husband and the message of any human being, regardless of their creed, belief and place of residence. It is also the right of any human being or any living thing – the right to live together with his family, with his children, and not to be prevented from doing so by anybody or any power.

In every country of the world, and in every human society, this matter seems to be the simplest of human rights that human beings enjoy. However, in Palestine, the situation is different as we live under the will of an Occupation that aspires to expel us from our nation, from our land, and in order to achieve this aim uses the ugliest and most oppressive means and uses all kinds of excuses to make us suffer and make our life more difficult. The repressive

Abdul Wahab Sabbah with Eelia

ABDUL WAHAB SABBAH, 2005

practices of the Occupation touch every Palestinian citizen wherever he is. The Occupation has become a curse that is pursuing us from birth to death.

With regard to my personal suffering under this Occupation, I can't remember its beginning, as I was born in 1970, which was three years after the occupation of the West Bank and Jerusalem. I have lived all my life as all of my Palestinian compatriots, and I have not enjoyed one day of freedom – quite the opposite. I was arrested when I was sixteen years of age for no crime but for reasons that I don't know until now – security reasons were cited. I was prevented from completing my education outside the country for the same supposed security reasons, and for ten years I was forced to work and study in Jerusalem which is a few metres away from my town, by finding my way around checkpoints – I did not ever get a permit that allowed me to enter Jerusalem legally.

The big problem started when the Occupation forces started building the racist Separation Wall around Jerusalem. Since 2003, my wife and children have been forced to move out of Abu Dis and live on the Western side of the Wall in East Jerusalem, as she has a Jerusalem identity card (Israeli), and my children were registered on her ID. This was the only way of being able to keep in touch with her family and work in East Jerusalem. I remained in Abu Dis as I couldn't have a permit to live with my children in East Jerusalem, despite the fact that I – like the rest of my generation from Abu Dis – was born in East Jerusalem

I know that this is a fairly common problem as many Palestinian families are suffering from separation in the West Bank. I know a lot of the international community accept the security excuse with which Israel justifies its repressive practices against the Palestinian people. But at the same time I know that I was deprived of the simplest of my human rights that has been guaranteed and called for in all religions and international conventions – my right to live with my children and my family in one house. For more than two years I have been prevented from settling. I only meet with my family once a week on Fridays and on Eid festivals, despite the fact that it is only the cursed Wall that separates us. I have tried repeatedly to approach the Israeli official circles, to get a permit or the right of residence in Jerusalem, but until now I have had any success.

Dear sirs, the dream of any Palestinian was to never give up our Palestinian national identity, and my people have made great sacrifices to keep our Palestinian national identity, so I do not want the price for keeping in touch with my family and children to be giving up my Palestinian national identity and exchanging it for an Israeli identity card, even if I were permitted to get it. I am asking for my right to enter the city in which I was born and where I was brought up, my right to be with my family, to look after them and provide for them. I don't think I am asking for the moon, and I don't care about the racist laws that were created by the Occupation while the international conventions have given me this right. Therefore I am writing to you to seek your help in applying what the nations and people have agreed to, and the messages God has given to people.

I ask you to provide me with the basic rights to work, to move freely and to live with my family according to the international conventions and accepted law.

With thanks.
Yours sincerely

Abdul Wahab Sabbah
Abu Dis, November 2005

Above right: Waiting to pass through a checkpoint to get to Abu Dis

Below right: Checkpoint turnstile – on the far side are Israeli soldiers

A call for help

DAR EL - TIFL

Phone 6283251 , P.O.B. 19377

JERUSALEM

مؤسسة
دار الطفل العربي
القدس
تأسست عام ١٣٦٧هـ / ١٩٤٨
تلفون : ٦٢٨٢٢٥١ - ص.ب ١٩٣٧٧
القدس

Date: 27-6-2005

To: Mr. Ali Abu Hilal,
Jerusalem Center for Democracy & Human Rights

Subject:The West Bank Identity holders employees working in Jerusalem.

Everybody knows that East Jerusalem , the axiomatic legal capital of Palestine, has been subject to a very vicious and constant attack by the Israeli Government to make it a Jewish city , despite its illegitimacy and against all the UN resolutions and against the wishes of the world body, yet Israel is proceeding in its procedures to transform East Jerusalem into a Jewish city. One of these measures is to isolate East Jerusalem and separate it from it neighbouring villages and cities by forbidding those who have West Bank identity card or better known those with green IDs from entering East Jerusalem.This affects mostly the employees who work in the Jerusalem schools. These employees and teachers have been working for years in the Jerusalem schools, and now they want to cut them off from their employment and source of income for the sole reason that they are green ID. holders.

There are many Palestinian Organizations, Institutes and Schools in Jerusalem who suffer the atrocities of the Israeli occupation against those with the green ID.cards, who are prevented to enter Jerusalem .If the organization or the employers of these employees are caught, they will pay heavy fines and are threatened with imprisonment , in addition to what these employees face at the check posts from humiliation, bad treatment and sending them back home, depriving the schools from receiving any teaching when their banned teachers are away for how many days, God knows .

Our Institute, Dar Al-Tifel Al-Arabi is one of these institutes and NGO organizations which employs a number of experienced and well-fledged administrators, teachers and employees who are now subject to expulsion from the D.T.A. Institute for the sole reason of being green ID. holders and live in the West Bank.

On behalf of all the green ID holders at D.T.A Institute , we forward this petition asking you to help us solve this predicament as it means depriving us from our employment and source of income. We want you to take the necessary measures to pressure the Israelies to grand us permits to enter East Jerusalem without fear of banning us from going to our work and to make our case known to all concerned authorities.

Thanking you for any effort you will do to support this vital problem that we face.

To contact us Tel: 026283251   Fax: 6273477   Email: info@dartifl.org

Respectfully yours,
DTA Employees

Out of work

I am 36 years old, and I used to work in the YMCA hotel in Jerusalem. I worked there for ten years, but it became very difficult after the Israelis built the Wall and the last time I managed to go to Jerusalem was three years ago.

Life is very tough and hard specially for the Palestinian workers, and specially the people who used to work in Jerusalem. It was always difficult but it became much harder when the Israelis started to build the Wall which separates the families from each other and the workers from their work and their students from their schools. It is making a very bad economic situation for all the Palestinian people, and now there is a very high level of unemployment.

Palestinian people have started to call to the outside world for help, but this help does not even cover the basic needs. If we could work it would not be needed. Tourism used to be extremely important in Palestine – work and the economy in Palestine have depended on it. But the Israeli procedures and specially this Wall they have built has made it very hard for this to continue.

Actually, tourism in Palestine stopped completely 8 years ago at the beginning of the second intifada, which stopped nearly all the main hotels and the tourist places from working, and in the Arab hotels in Jerusalem so many workers lost their jobs. In the past, there were hundreds of workers who used to work in Jerusalem and in the hotels, but now nearly all of them have lost their work because of the Israeli procedures.

I wish that all these problems would stop to give us as workers a chance to return back to our work in Jerusalem.

Since that time, I have been out of work and the main reason for that is the Wall and because of the Israeli system. They did not give us permits to enter Jerusalem.

Now I am working hard to create a small business just to try to help my family, even if it will never be enough to cover our expenses, and anyway it won't solve the general problem – now, thousands of workers don't have the means to live.

TALAL YOUNIS ABU HILAL, 2008

Studying at Al Quds University

I am a student at the Al Quds University in Abu Dis. I come from Bethlehem but I travel to Al Quds to study in the Gender Studies Department there.

Students in Palestine have lots of problems and some of the main ones are checkpoints. You never know when there will be a checkpoint. There is a fixed checkpoint on the road from Bethlehem to Abu Dis called the Container Checkpoint. Every day it is very slow at the times that people are on their way to work or on their way back. The soldiers shut the checkpoint and they go inside and listen to music. They don't check anything but they don't let you move, and it can be for a very long time. The main reason they have checkpoints is to make life hard for you.

Soldiers stop you at checkpoints whenever they want to. There are also 'flying checkpoints', which means

Below: Rawan (centre) on a student visit to Britain, organised by CADFA

Below right: Al Quds University campus, Abu Dis

RAWAN ABU AMREYEH, MARCH 2008

temporary checkpoints on the road. In Abu Dis, the main place they do this is on the road to the university and the main people that they delay are students. They can take your ID away for a long time. The thing that is difficult is not knowing if there is going to be a checkpoint or how long it will hold you up.

Students are often late for lectures because it is hard to know how long a journey will take. One time, I completely missed my exam. I was really worried, and when I went to tell my teacher that I had been held up at a checkpoint, at first he didn't believe me, he thought it was just an excuse. In the end though they let me do it late. It is really stressful.

There are lots of other pressures on students under occupation. One thing is prison – there are about seventy students from Al Quds in prison at the moment. Earlier this year, they arrested the head of the student council. They often arrest young men at the checkpoints on the road to the university. In fact young men miss years of their education this way – some of

them are arrested when they are at school, and some when they are at university – it can happen at any time, and maybe that is one of the reasons why there are more girls at Al Quds University than boys (there are 60% girls).

Our university is right next to the Separation Wall which goes through its land. This divides our campus from the part in Jerusalem and it is very difficult. The university had to move its main door to the other side of the building because of the Wall. The main library is on the other side and a lot of us (like me) can't go there. The Wall is changing everything – where people can work, where they can study, who they can see. It also goes round my town Bethlehem and is ruining the tourism industry which is very old and very important to the town.

The army on the streets after school

On Wednesday 14th February, after the end of the day, after the sixth class, at about 1.30pm, we went out of our school. Then I and my friends heard that the Israeli army had invaded Abu Dis Boys' School earlier that day, which made us very nervous because we knew that they stopped a day of education at that school. It was very hard for us to hear that they entered the classrooms and they beat the students and the teachers. The thing that also added to the misery was that when we went out, the soldiers were waiting for the students, because they wanted to arrest students who had thrown stones.

While my friends and I were walking on the road from the school, an Israeli jeep stopped us. The soldiers got out and started to ask us questions. One soldier asked me whether I had thrown stones, and he was shouting, and another soldier asked a friend of mine the same question, and he hit my friend on his head.

After that, the soldiers got in their car and they went, leaving the children who had been beaten and humiliated without any exact reason except they were on the road between school and home – this makes education dangerous in our country.

MOHÁMMED HASSAN ABU HILAL, 2007
A student from the Arab Institute, Abu Dis

The army outside the school

NADEEM KHALIL ABU HILAL, 2007
Abu Dis Boys' School

I am writing to you to talk about a serious problem which we had in our school on our way to continue our education. The main problem is the Israeli army which is around our school all the time, and if we enter our school they lock us inside or even sometimes before we enter our school, they close the doors and refuse to allow us to enter.

That's what happened on Saturday 24th March 2007 at about 11.30 in the morning. There were soldiers at the front door of the school and they refused to allow us to go out of the school. The students were very afraid of the soldiers and none of them came near the main door.

The soldiers stayed there, and their military vehicle stayed there in front of the school. They were fully armed and they aimed their weapons at the main door of the school. Although our teachers tried to talk to the soldiers, asking them to leave the place and allow the students to go home, the soldiers refused. So the teachers made their bodies into a fence between the students and the Israeli soldiers, and they managed to protect us and let us go out of the school.

But still, even when we left the school, one of the soldiers started to run after the children on the streets on their way home.

The army inside the school

ASEM AWAD, FEBRUARY 2007
Asem Awad Is the Abu Dis Boys' School guard

Abu Dis Boys' School has now raised the money from parents and others to put up a metal grille to protect the boys against further invasions by Israeli soldiers

While I was sitting near the main gate of the school, at the break time, the Israeli Border Police came from behind the school, and from near the main door of the school a stone was thrown at them. They shook the gate very strongly and they entered the school and without any mercy they started to attack the students with their wooden sticks.

The children were trying to explain to the soldiers that they were innocent and they were not trying to do anything, but they attacked them, they did not give them any opportunity to defend themselves. They beat them on their hands and on their legs. Although one of the teachers tried to help the children, they also beat him on his right shoulder.

The headteacher of the school came to the soldiers and they threatened to blow up the school if anything happened in the future, in other words if anyone threw stones. The headteacher managed to get them out of the school after a sharp argument, asking them why they had beaten the children and the teachers.

This is not fair, it is not legal for soldiers to enter the school like this. I was very afraid because we have a disabled child and I worried about him, thank God they did not beat him.

That was what I saw.

Al Marfa' Centre for Psychological Health

MOUSA NAJIB, 2008

Mohammed
Hassan

We created this centre in 2003 as a direct result of the Wall being built. We believe the Wall caused major psychological damage to the people of the towns of East Jerusalem. Because the special relation between the people of this area and their city was something nobody expected to lose. It was not easy for anybody just to imagine inside himself that he would never go to Jerusalem again. Also, and as all the other health services, psychological services used to be in Jerusalem for the people of these towns. And now after the city was cut from the suburbs, Abu Dis needs such a service.

The Wall

From my own experience with the society here, I feel that people are suffering exile in their own land because of the loss of Jerusalem. Even for me myself, when I stand near the Wall, looking at this ugly thing that prevents me from reaching the place that is the heart of my life, I feel hugely disappointed.

Children under Occupation

One of the big problems that the centre deals with is that people in Abu Dis in general, and particularly children, do not have any specific role or plan for their future. An example of this, a child who is thirteen years old asked a question "What is the meaning of peace without justice?" This shows how these children are actually involved in the Palestinian pain. We are working with them just to make them believe in the future and to have optimistic view about their own lives, which is not easy for them or us under all this pressure that we live in.

We also deal a lot with teenage rebellion, and the issue of disobedience and lack of respect for their parents. Any child in the world believes that his father is the strongest man in the world and respects his father because his father has a great value for him. Because of what is happening here, especially when this child sees his father humiliated and his house invaded by soldiers, or finds that his father does not have the chance to work, this affects the relationship between the father and the son very badly. It is very hard to control the anger of these teenagers, at a time when there is no other useful thing to do, there is no chance for these children to live their childhood, there are no special places for them to go.

We are working on building psychological resilience and we are trying to create an optimistic side inside the new generation, through opening a wide door for them to express themselves. So far we have managed to work on very useful programmes for youths.

Mothers of prisoners

Another important issue we are dealing with is a special programme for the mothers of the prisoners. We discovered that they have a continuous deep fear inside themselves and they are worried all the time. These psychological effects can lead to physical disease. They ask questions about their children, what will happen with their future, thinking that somehow they could have protected their children and blaming themselves for not having managed to. This also affects all the members of their families, specially the other children in the house, so damage related to this can reach each member of that family.

Child prisoners

We also deal with child prisoners. A very short period for any child inside Israeli jail can change the life of this child or make him grow up without having a chance to enjoy his childhood.

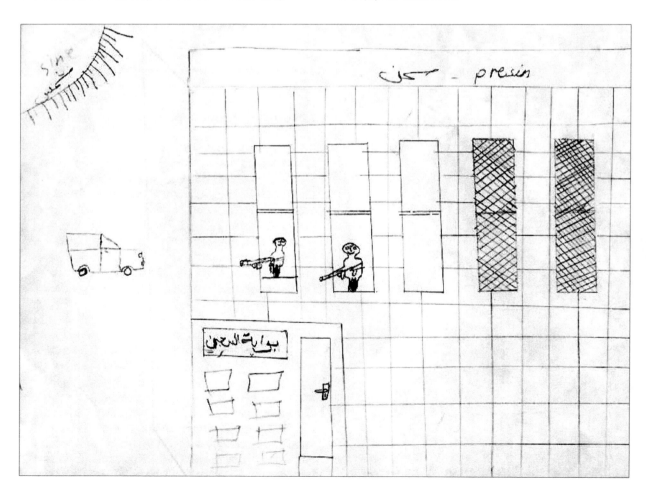

Israeli soldiers on the rampage

REPORT FROM ABU DIS DECEMBER 2007

**Israeli soldiers beating Ahmed Eriqat in the street in Abu Dis, 11 December 07.
Photo taken at risk by a schoolboy with his mobile phone**

This report is made from the combined statements from a number of people from Abu Dis

On Tuesday evening, December 11th 2007, a CADFA volunteer living near the middle of town wrote "it is extremely noisy outside – there has been shooting, screaming sirens, just at the end of my road." Others in Abu Dis reported panic and chaos everywhere with the army going around all night, and soldiers saying "Abu Dis will not sleep tonight." There were roadblocks, shooting and chaos. One person returning from work in Ramallah said that it wasn't possible for him to get home: he had to sleep under a tree.

At about 8.30 in the evening the trouble started and soldiers from the military camp burst into a house in Ras al Aqub. At about the same time, five Israeli jeeps from the military camp drove into town with sirens wailing and lights flashing. Four soldiers entered two supermarkets, one after another, told them to close and ordered the owners to stay inside. They broke the front windows of the Eriqat shop (and later they broke others).

There were a lot of people in the cafés because there was a football match that night. Soldiers entered the Beatles Café violently. They broke a very big mirror and hit the glass door of the cafe hard with their weapons (but it did not break). They pushed, hit and kicked the café customers. They ordered dozens of men to go outside and stand next to the wall with hands raised above their heads and they collected their IDs. Later the Palestinian men were forced to sit in a squatting position, still with their hands above their heads, which is very hard for people to do especially for a long time. The soldiers remained about an hour near the café. Eight soldiers went on foot to the university crossroads, ordering owners to close their shops and stay inside.

According to witnesses, 21-year-old Ahmed Radi Eriqat, brother of the owner Mohammed, was working in the petrol station nearby. Soldiers told him to lock it and stay inside. Three soldiers came and broke the glass shopfront of the shop next door, so Ahmed came out to see what was happening. At this point, the soldiers attacked him, then pushed Ahmed into the shop along with Abdullah Dawoud Awad (28 years old, shop owner) and started beating them both. We have been sent these pictures of blood on a shelf in the shop and on the shop floor which came from the attack on the young men.

After beating them for fifteen minutes, the soldiers dragged the two young men outside and along the street. When they reached the shop of Abdullah Lafee they started beating them again, outside the door of the shop, knocking Ahmed's head against the door. Until he heard screaming and realized what was happening, Abdullah Lafee assumed that the sound was the soldiers knocking at his door. Abdullah Awad's mother who lived nearby went to the soldiers and tried to intervene to protect her son and his neighbour, but the soldiers simply pushed her away. At 9.45 the soldiers forced Ahmed and Abdullah into a military jeep, handcuffed and blindfolded.

The two families got into cars and followed the jeep which went to the military camp in Abu Dis, but the Israeli soldiers refused to allow the families to enter. After about half an hour, the soldiers left with the two men and took them to Maale Adumim police station. The families followed and managed to enter the police station. They saw their sons at a distance with their eyes blindfolded and their hands tied behind their backs, but they did not manage to communicate with them.

Abdullah's brother tried to talk to the police officer about these events, not only about his brother but about the damage to his shop. He was told that nothing would be done unless there was some evidence, so he returned to collect photos and film which were sent to a lawyer to start a formal complaint.

At 10.30 the soldiers returned to the area of Abudullah's shop and made a deliberate sound explosion. This seemed to be a pretence at detonating a suspicious package to suggest that the issue was the fault of the local people.

After this, Israeli soldiers invaded the Jaffa Café and again violently forced dozens of people to go outside and hand over their IDs The soldiers also damaged some of the interior of the café, destroying six shishas. At 11 p.m. some soldiers returned with the ID cards for everyone, including the people still waiting outside the Beatles Café, and threw them on to the ground.

At 1 am, two Israeli jeeps returned to Abdullah Awad's shop and told his brother that the glass had been broken by Palestinians throwing stones. There was a car tyre burning in the street near the shop. No one knew who had put it there. The soldiers took photos of the burning tyre and the shop and said that the local people were responsible for the trouble.

One of the soldiers left the jeep, jumped over a fence and returned to the street with two Molotov cocktails which he claimed to have found – again seeming to be trying to show that it was the locals causing the damage. This was after the complaint had been made at the police station in Maale Adumim.

Residents of the old neighbourhood of Abu Dis said that at 1am soldiers came again, throwing sound bombs, knocking on doors and making a great noise to wake everyone up. They let off sound bombs throughout the evening which seemed to have no reason except to make people afraid and stop them sleeping.

Ahmed and Abdullah were both hurt badly by the beating, and later were each charged with attacking a soldier, put in prison for 5 months and given a fine of 3000 shekels each.

The martyr Fadi Baher

KHAMEES MOHAMMED RABIYEH, 14 YEARS OLD
2006

Fadi Baher, aged 19, was killed outside Abu Dis Youth Club on 10th May 2004

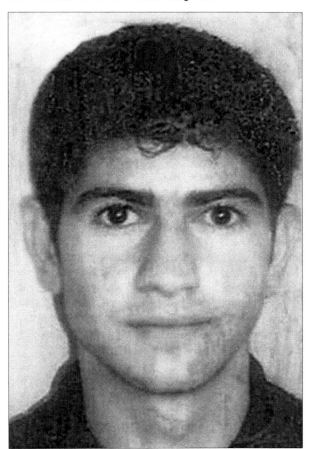

"Beloved Palestine, how shall I sleep
With ghosts of sadness in my eyes?"

Don't I have the right to live in security? Don't I have the right to practise my hobbies? Doesn't a young Palestinian youth have the right to a peaceful country, like the rest of the world? Isn't it the right of Palestinian children not to have a father in prison or a brother a martyr like Fadi?

Why was Fadi killed?

Fadi, one of the Palestinian youth, was playing sport in Abu Dis Youth Club when he went out from the club, he and his friends. There was a Border Police car, and the occupier aimed his lethal bullets at Fadi's head. When they realised that Fadi was still clinging on to life, they drove their car over him, and when the ambulance came, the occupiers didn't let the ambulance take Fadi, who became a martyr to the land of Palestine, the land of martyrs.

When his brother heard of the martyrdom, he went to see, but found him a martyr – and the occupation soldiers weren't satisfied with killing Fadi – they aimed their rubber weapons in the direction of his brother and arrested him.

Hasn't the time come for us to feel freedom and security?

The killing of Maryam Ayyad

On Saturday 20th September 2008, Maryam Ayyad, 58 years old, was killed by Israeli border police, when dozens of them invaded her house which is on the University Street in Abu Dis. The soldiers closed the University Street with two checkpoints and then entered Maryam's house.

Hiba Ayyad, Maryam's youngest daughter, was with her when she was killed. She said, "My mother was killed by the occupation. The soldiers who killed her in cold blood did not even allow the ambulance to reach her. Dozens of soldiers came to the house to arrest a student from Al Quds University who lives in a room in our building. When the soldiers tried to go upstairs in the building, where my brother Nasser lives with his wife and children, my mother tried to stop them and told them that there were children in this house, and they were asleep. None of the soldiers listened, and one of them pushed my mother on to the ground."

[Her mother was clearly very seriously hurt.]

"Right away I tried to go out to the street, shouting to the neighbours, asking them to bring an ambulance to save my mother. One of the soldiers pointed his gun at me and forced me to return back inside the house.

"Our neighbours called the ambulance, but at the same time, the soldiers told me that my mother was dead. I did not believe it, because everything happened quickly."

From her nephew:

"I just wanted to tell you that Maryam Ayyad is my aunt, the sister of my father. My father just told me that at the night this whole thing happened, after he heard about what happened, he rushed outside and then he took our neighbour Dr.Ahmad Abed al Kareem with him, then they left together in the car and when they got there the Israeli troops prevented then from entering the area and they did the same thing with the ambulance. After they made sure that she was dead they let them in.

"She was so kind, she was a basic thing in our lives. What I want to say is that she was like a mother to me and that I used to visit her every day after school and I'd like to add that after she left she left a big empty hole in my life ..."

"From the heart, being the brother of
Mariam Ahmad Ayyad, we appreciate the
lovely touches you put about our sister
Mariam Ayyad, UMM NASSER. I would like
to present this photo of my family in 2005,
June 25th, at the time of my visit to Abu Dis
from the USA.
Mariam Ayyad, wearing Black."

Maryam's brother, Sammy Ahmad Ayyad

A present for
Eid-al-Fitr

REPORT FROM ABU DIS, MAY 2007

Dear friends in Camden

Abu Dis has received a present for Eid-al-Fitr from the Occupation. Around 4 am early in the morning today, the Occupation army and Israeli intelligence forces attacked a group of houses in Abu Dis and arrested four young people from the town.

They forced their way into our house and took my father outside the house to inspect his identity card while they searched the building. Later it was clear that they were searching for the son of our neighbour, one of our relatives, who wasn't there when they were there. Unfortunately I couldn't take photos because the situation was very dangerous.

They threatened that they would shoot in the door of the son's flat if the door wasn't opened. The truth is that he wasn't in the building. If it wasn't for his mother who had the key to the flat it wouldn't have been possible to persuade them that he was not there.

I'm going out now to enquire about the arrested people and to comfort my friends.

Photo from Abu Jihad Museum of Political Prisoners, Abu Dis

My son in prison

My son is Ibrahim Jaffal. He is 17 years old.

On 19th February, 2006, he was arrested. 15 young men were arrested on the same night. The Israeli army knocked on the door very very loud. There was no chance to open the door. They broke it.

They took the young men to Maale Adumim police station. They blindfolded them.

They didn't know where they were. The soldier asked them if they knew where they were. There was a big sound of people shouting. My son is strong. He said, "I am in a hospital and women are giving birth."

They took him to Awfar Jail. He hasn't had a trial.

I am going to visit him next Wednesday. We go in the Red Cross buses. We go at 6 o'clock in the morning and wait. Maybe we see them in the afternoon. Between us and them there are two barriers made of metal with little holes. It is very difficult to hear them. No way to touch each other.

We can stay for 45 minutes. They let us take photos of them if there are small brothers and sisters, but my son is the last one and we can't take photos.

Another prisoner, Mohammed Saleh Mohsen: photo taken in prison, with his parents. Mohammed has been in prison for years; now he has cancer but his parents are not allowed to visit him

IM IBRAHIM JAFFAL, NOVEMBER 2006

Arrested

يا دامي الحَزِينَ والنَّكينَ إنَّ اللَّيلَ
نَ أئل لا غرفَة التَّحقِيق باقِيَة وَلا زَرْدَ

MAJDI SALAH, 17 YEARS OLD
2007

I was arrested on Wednesday 26th April 2007 from my house at 12:30am. Six Israeli military vehicles and fifteen soldiers arrived at the house. They knocked forcefully on the door and my father answered. The intelligence officer asked my father about his sons. My father said that two of them were already inside Israeli jails, one of them was away visiting his fiancée, and that Majdi, the fourth, was asleep. The Intelligence Officer asked my father to bring Majdi to him. When I came the Officer asked me about my ID, and he told me to go and get dressed and ready to leave with him. They took me from the house and put a blindfold over my eyes and tied up my hands.

They then put me on the floor inside the jeep. There were three soldiers surrounding me. The vehicles went down to the old neighbourhood of Abu Dis. The other vehicles went to another house and they arrested somebody else and then all the vehicles continued to Ma'ale Adumim Police Station.

I and the other person who was arrested, who I could not see, were taken to wait in a room in the Police Station with soldiers all around us. One hour later they came and took me to a dark room. I was still blindfolded and tied up at this point. I was not allowed to sit down. There were two investigators in the room. I did not manage to see them very well, but from under the blindfold I could see that they were wearing military uniforms.

The investigators began to threaten me. They told me: "We have two ways of working with you. First, you can give us all the information we want from you and we will deal with you as a human being, or second, you will face a very hard time here."

The first question was whether I had thrown stones at a jeep or not. I said that I had not thrown stones. The officer began to use his knee to hit me in my thigh. After that he pushed me and I fell down on the ground. He started to beat me and kick me. He hit me on my back and between my legs, this lasted about fifteen minutes. After that he asked me to stand up. He continued to question me but before I had a chance to answer he began to beat me round my head. This process continued for more than one hour, maybe an hour and a half.

After this, he took me to another room, this time it was lit. The officer said that he had proof that I was throwing stones, he started to give me the names of other children in Abu Dis, claiming that these children had already confessed and that they had mentioned my name. I took the blindfold off my eyes and looked him in the eye. He became very angry and started to beat me again.

After this he put the blindfold over my eyes again and tied it tightly. Then he asked me to sign a piece of paper, and I refused to sign this paper. He began again to beat me around the head and shouted at me, saying bad things about my mother and my god. He used a container made out of heavy card to beat me directly around the head. I told him that I couldn't sign and so the soldier said that I should give him my thumbprint as a signature. I refused this also. At this point the soldier said: "I will send you outside to the soldiers and they will beat you up and kill you".

He also threatened to use electric shocks on me if I didn't sign. When I refused he brought a cable and made me hold it. I said that I didn't care- he could put the cable anywhere on my body. So he put it between the blindfold and my head. When he saw that I was not afraid he hit me in the face and sent me outside to the soldiers. Two soldiers took my hands and they started to walk me away and make jokes about me. Then they took me and the other boy they had arrested to another jeep. I sat on the floor and the other prisoner sat on the ammunition box. We were taken to the military camp in Abu Dis.

When we arrived at the military camp it was nearly four o' clock in the morning. They put us outside, it was very cold. We stayed there for nearly three hours in the same position until about seven o'clock in the morning. Then they took us to Kfar Atzioun which is a settlement in the south of Bethlehem.

I was taken to a room where there was a woman with a military uniform. She took my blood pressure and my temperature. After that they took me to the jail. We were forced to stand facing a fence from eight thirty until one o' clock in the afternoon. Then they took us inside the jail. They removed everything from our pockets, IDs, cigarettes, our watches, and

then they sent me to one of the rooms. After an hour we were brought some food. This was the first thing we had eaten since we were arrested. It was rice crawling with insects. We just ate bread and water. Also inside this room there was no toilet. After we ate we were taken outside for fifteen minutes to go to the toilet.

There was no bed inside the room, just a small thin plastic sheet. At ten o clock at night we were brought our supper. This was cold spaghetti and an egg which was blue inside.

I spent seven days inside this jail. During this time I only ate bread and water. We were given four cigarettes a day each. One day I was punished because I spent more than five minutes in the bathroom. This day I was not given cigarettes. The room had twelve prisoners inside. There was only one small window which was covered in steel so that we could not see daylight. The light was left permanently on, even at night.

There were insects in the room all the time so we couldn't sleep. The only health treatment we were allowed to receive during this time was aspirin.

After seven days they called me outside to the main office and asked me to call my family, to ask them to pay 2500 shekels to Ma'ale Adumim police station in order to be released. The next day my family went to Ma'ale Adumim and negotiated with the police. In the end, they paid 1500 shekels to release me.

While my family were paying the money, a police officer came to the room in the jail and called my name. He said that I had been given administrative detention for six months. I was very upset and returned back to my room in the jail.

Then the same officer called me back and said that I was 'mad' and that I must go back home. They asked me to go to Ma'ale Adumim police station the same day. I was then released.

When I went to the police station, the police officers gave me a written order to go to the court on the 30th of July.

Nakba march

Some of the families, teachers and Al Quds University students in Abu Dis joined representatives of public bodies in the town in a public march to commemorate 60 years of the Palestinian Nakba .

The children on the march carried model heads painted with wide-open eyes and ears but firmly-shut mouths, to symbolise the world that could see and hear everything that was happening to the Palestinians but was silent and impotent. They carried placards demanding the right to return for the Palestinian refugees, and calling for national unity.

The march ended at the racist Separation Wall next to the Al Quds University, and there the marchers painted keys representing return, and wrote poems on the wall. Some of the poems were read out and some national songs were sung. After the event, the marchers visited the Abu Jihad Museum for Palestinian Prisoners and presented the museum with the model heads that they had been carrying.

REPORT FROM ABU DIS, 15TH MAY 2008

Palestinian: you are not allowed to live

BELAL MOHSEN, 2007

Palestinian – not allowed to live

They tell you to shut up and not say anything

You were born to be beaten up

Checkpoints, terminals, searches

Have written on your forehead "To be stepped on"

By the officer and by the sergeant

They tell you, Palestinian, you are not allowed to live

Palestinian, you are not allowed to resist

And you are not allowed to say you are oppressed

Don't ask for your rights

In the daytime you are not to see the light

* * * * * *

Not allowed to renew your ID card

Not allowed to renew your passport

Palestinian, and you want to learn?!

Well, that is against the law

Palestinian you must feel pain

But you are not allowed to see the doctor

Palestinian you are not allowed to complain

And your wings are not to grow feathers

To live, Palestinian, is forbidden.

* * * * * *

Palestinian, in every airport

Your name is written in red

And on the windows of the passport authority

Have written on your forehead "Wanted"

You have to wait hours

Guilty without doing anything wrong

And they present you with charges:

– You are the reason for all the wars

As if, because of you, right died

And justice has been taken from your land

As if you are the cause of all the calamities

And all the crises people have

And as if because of you, a murderer went

To Jenin at the moment of sunset

And slaughtered the boys and the girls

– while you can't do anything to stop these.

* * * * * *

Well in truth

I am the victim of the world

You made me the subject of songs

The cause of people with no cause of their own

My head is not going to bend

When I face a strong wind

I am from a steadfast people

In the West Bank and in Rashidya camp

I am from a people who resist

With a stone against a military unit

And today and tomorrow and forever

We have something to say, which is

* * * * * *

Palestine is Arab

And it is going to stay Arab

And Arab it is going to stay.

CADFA work
in Abu Dis

Letter to Camden Councillors

Cllr Mohammed Eid is a Councillor from Abu Dis Town Council who came on a CADFA visit to Camden in November 2007. Camden Abu Dis Friendship Association organise several visits a year for people from Abu Dis to Camden. The purpose of these visits is to make links with different groups in Camden and create awareness about the human rights situation in Abu Dis

Re The current situation and continuous suffering in Abu Dis and the work of Camden Abu Dis Friendship Association

Greetings and respect.

I want to tell you some of the main points about the problems in Abu Dis that result from the current situation.

Abu Dis is a very old town, near Jerusalem. It has always been related to Jerusalem. We have ancient Roman remains. It has always been the eastern door into Jerusalem. It used to depend on on agriculture and grazing on the land on the east, which stretched to the Dead Sea. Abu Dis people have ownership documents up to now for this land.

As any Palestinian town, Abu Dis has been influenced enormously by the Occupation, especially Israel's pressure on Abu Dis people to move from Jerusalem in order to extend the settlements such as Maale Adumim and the small settlements around it which were established on the hilltops around Abu Dis on our Abu Dis land.

In Abu Dis, we have just received military orders to take away further land on the north-west and south-east of Abu Dis.

Abu Dis is surrounded on all sides: on the north and the west by the wall. The east has always been Abu Dis' direction of expansion – the last chance of expansion but is closed by the settlements under construction now, and on the south by the Container checkpoint.

MOHAMMED EID, 2007

The growing number of people, now 13,000, live in 460 donums of land. Less than 40% are suitable for building because of the steep nature of the land. You have also to add to the number the students and staff of Al Quds University which contains more than 1100 students and staff, 60% of whom live in Abu Dis.

In Abu Dis at the moment, we have seen the outputs of Camden Abu Dis Friendship , which has links now in many sectors, education, health etc, and we believe that through the associations like this we can bring our voice to the outside world. These days we are meeting with Camden Abu Dis Friendship Association, and their work is well-known to Abu Dis Council. We are pleased to work with them because we have seen tangible results and we very much hope to push this forward.

My visit here will be very valuable to other members of Abu Dis council, and I will tell them what has happened to me and tell them that it is important to help the Association to grow and develop.

I hope that you will also be able to assist this association in order to achieve their goals in human rights for Abu Dis people, specially the right to life, the right to travel, the right to have education etc.

We are looking for your understanding.

Mohammed Eid
Councillor, Abu Dis Town Council

November 2007

Special day for diabetic patients at Camden Clinic, Abu Dis

Letters from the schools

FROM ABU DIS BOYS' SCHOOL
AND AQEL ABU KHALIL, 2007

Below:
Camden teacher in Abu Dis school

Below right: Abu Dis students in Camden school

CADFA and Camden Abu Dis Education Links have developed good relations with all the schools in Abu Dis through our visits of teachers in both directions and schoolchildren from Abu Dis to London [1]. CADFA has helped Abu Dis schools in a number of practical ways and also gave support in February 2007, when Abu Dis School boys were beaten in their classrooms by Israeli soldiers.
In November 2007, the school twinned with Hampstead School in Camden , which proved to be the first in a number of Camden-Abu Dis school twinnings.[2]

ABU DIS BOYS' SCHOOL

We extend our gratitude for all the efforts
that you have made in regard to the
event of February 14th and the way Israeli
soldiers acted in Abu DIs School. We
highly appreciate all your endeavours that
came out with good results. The Israeli
Authorities heard from the Headmaster
and investigated their soldiers who entered
the school and were hostile against the
boys, and we believe, thanks to your
efforts, this will be a lesson for them and
we hope that it won't be done again to our
school. Moreover, we have received with
great pleasure your offer of establishing a
twinning programme between our school
and another one from Britain. We are very
enthusiastic about this idea and we look
forward to hear more about it from you.
So, we can't wait to get more information
about this cooperation programme. (Aqel)

ARAB INSTITUTE, ABU DIS

We would sincerely like to thank… the Camden
Abu Dis Friendship Association in London for their
interesting visit with a number of volunteers the the
Arab Institute School in October 2007 … No doubt that
the visit is useful and both Camden's teachers and the
Institute's teachers have exchanged the educational
experiences which lead to improve the academic and
psychological environment for our students.

At the Arab Institute, we are so glad to have links
with Camden, via the volunteers, visits and teachers'
exchanges and we look forward to strengthening
these links in the future. (Ali)

FOOTNOTES

[1] www.camdenabudis.net See education and visits
[2] http://abudisboyschool.blogspot.com

Women's group at Dar Assadaqa, Abu Dis

NADIA ABU REDA, APRIL 2008

The women's group is one of the groups that work in the Dar Assadaqa Community Centre, one of the projects that CADFA supports in Abu Dis. For more information on the women's activities see www.camdenabudis.net/women or on Dar Assadaqa see the Dar Assadaqa blog: http://darassadaqa.blogspot.com

I want to talk about why I am part of the women's group in Dar Assadaqa andI am on the committee.

I am really happy with the women's group because I feel that it plays a very important role in our local community. And for women, all the programmes that we have had in the past two years have helped women to educate themselves and raised the level of women's participation in the community in Abu Dis.

For me, this was something new. It gave me a good chance to meet with the community in Abu Dis, specially the women. I am living in Abu Dis but my family is not from here so these activities have given me a chance to make friends. I have learned a lot from courses in English, computer and first aid, all these different things, and also I learned a lot about the situation of the community through this relation with Dar Assadaqa women's committee.

This relation with CADFA and with people in Camden and in London has shown us, as the Palestinian people, that there are people who care about us and stand next to us in Abu Dis. We know that CADFA is working hard to raise awareness and highlight about the Palestinian sufferings in general and the life of people under occupation.

We know that our friends in Camden are working all the time on this. I took part in a visit to Camden last year and was part of demonstrations and different activities. In fact, I felt that I was not away from my homeland because of all the friendly people that I met; I am proud that I met these people and I know them. I hope that this relation will continue because this is one important way for us as Palestinians to send our message about our suffering to the whole world.

Also CADFA has had a very important role in sending different groups of people to visit Abu Dis, and finding volunteers for us here, which is a very good and serious thing for us.

We consider that these people who come here and live with us under this pressure of occupation will definitely be very useful when they return back, and they will talk about our issues. We have been involved in all the visits. Next month the Dar Assadaqa women's committee will host a delegation of women from Camden and we will be taking them to visit women's organisations across the West Bank.

During the past two years, the women's committee at Dar Assadaqa has worked on many different projects and activities for the local community and specially the women in Abu Dis. Our goal all the time is to have as many women in Abu Dis as possible sharing in these activities.

Some of our activities have been: courses in handcrafts together with a teacher from Bethlehem, a first aid course, a computer course, English courses

Some of the women's group on the steps of Dar Assadaqa

that the volunteers have been giving for
women over the past two years, counselling
courses, health education, films for women,
women's outings, making a newsletter. We
work with other groups, for example we work
with the Red Crescent to help the mothers of
prisoners. We have made newsletters about
our work.

We would like to try to find resources for income
to help the women in the local community to
develop their skills, so women can contribute to
the family income in this terrible crisis we have,
with the occupation and the economic crisis
following the building of the Wall.

For myself I really want to give something to
CADFA from myself as a response to the good
things that CADFA has done for me and for
Abu Dis people. I wonder if it is possible to
send volunteers from Abu Dis to teach Arabic
language in London.

To our friends in London

CADFA has done a lot of work with young people in Abu Dis, specially work that brings their voice to Camden. CADFA has supported the Dar Assadaqa youth group to work on film, music and dance and brought young people involved in these things to meet young people in Camden.

Written August 07 from Abu Dis

We would like to send our greetings to our friends in England and specially our friends in Camden, thanks for all their efforts and for the hard work they have done for us to make our visit succeed. We would like to thank all of you for the warm hospitality because we all of us felt that we were in our homeland and among our family. Also we want to thank all the friends who joined us during our programme.

The young people who came on the youth visit to Camden in July 07:

RASHA AL HREMI, SHEMA AREBEH, NADEEM ABU, HILAL, MOHAMMAD ABU HILAL, MOHAMMAD QUREIA, HUSSEIN BADR

As for the visit, we think that we managed to send the message that we went there for, through the meetings and the visits that we had with different organisations and clubs and associations. We tried to give a good picture about our citizens and our culture and the folklore of the Palestinian people. We hope that we managed to reflect a small part of our suffering and our struggle against the Israeli occupation. We had a very valuable opportunity to make a very nice relation with new friends and we can continue our connection with them through phone and internet.

Also we are very happy about the media covering our visit during all of our visit, because we managed to hold many meetings with the TV channels and newspapers and so on. This thing made it seem that our case become very important for the European people, and has been put in a spotlight.

Also one of the most important things that we

managed to discuss in this meeting is the case of child prisoners in Abu Dis. One of the most amazing things is Camden people adopting Abu Dis prisoners. We managed to discuss the Separation Wall and its terrible effects on the economic, social and political life of the Abu Dis people. One of the very nice things for us was that we took part in a demonstration in Camden Town against the Occupation and the Separation Wall.

We hope that we can get another opportunity to repeat such a visit to London to continue our relation with our friends. Also we hope that the next visit will be for Camden children to Abu Dis to feel the effect of the Occupation on Abu Dis children.

In the end we want to say thank you very much to all the people who helped us to be in London, specially our friends in Camden.

Support for my son

Rabiha's son Saif was seventeen, in his final year at school, when he was taken from his house by Israeli soldiers and put in prison. He spent fifteen months without a trial and in the end spent eighteen months in prison. His mother here is talking about the CADFA prisoner adoption programme

The feeling of support from this programme is very beautiful, it's great. When we are in a crisis, there are people walking with us, standing by us – this really helps the family and the prisoner.

I remember the letter that came to my son for my son's 18 birthday. It had 35 signatures on it. I am still keeping it till now and I am very proud of it. On the day it came, I spoke to Saif on the telephone in prison. He remembers now how much it encouraged him, that there are people that he didn't know who remembered his birthday and were in solidarity with him through all he was going through.

From my experience from the programme of adoption, it is very helpful, and other mothers of prisoners feel the same. From the point of view of Saif and all the prisoners who were around him, it was so good to know that he has friends who care about him and ask about him all the time.

Up to today, Saif has all the letters and he wants to communicate with people and thank them when he has finished his exams.

The programme is brilliant, but is there any chance of starting a new programme for these youths after they come back out of prison to help them link to their community again and get back to their lives, because it is a very difficult time for them?

RABIHA ABU HILAL 2008

A letter to CADFA

CADFA has worked with health professionals in Abu Dis on a number of projects, working with the Faisal al-Husseini Health Centre and the Al-Muqassed Centre and supporting the opening of a new out-of-hours and emergency clinic that was badly needed because of the Wall. This has been called the Camden Clinic.

But a solution to the health problems of people in Abu Dis does not lie purely in providing medical relief; CADFA also works to highlight the human rights violations that cause the problems.

FROM THE FAMILY OF SHEHADEH AHMED MOHSEN, 2006

Dear friends in Camden:

With greetings to all of you.

From the outset, we value your principled stand with the struggle of our people to gain its inalienable rights through your close and direct relationship with us in Abu Dis. We hope that this fruitful relationship will continue and become stronger as a result of our joint efforts to achieve this goal.

Oh friends, it is not the first time that one of Abu Dis sons falls martyr to the military checkpoints and through deadly attempts sometimes to get past the Separation Apartheid Wall that stops the sick from reaching their medical centres in Jerusalem. And before the last martyr, Shehadah Mohsen, many fell due to the Occupation Forces' deliberate prevention of these people reaching their hospitals.

And these martyrs from the old and those who have serious illnesses and whose health conditions did not help them to endure the unbearable circumstances, especially during the enormous summer heat and bitter winter cold that usually accompanies people moving from Abu Dis past the Wall. The problem now is that the Separation Wall is about to be finished, which means it will be impossible for any students to go to his school or the sick person to go to his medical centre. At the same time, the very few permits that some people used to get when they go to medication or study, have stopped – obtaining them is next to impossible – which means more suffering, deepening the crisis that Abu Dis and its surrounding areas suffer from.

Shehadeh Mohsen fell as a martyr. He was 55 years of age, and he was supposed to visit his medical centre, that is part of the Muqassed Hospital in Jerusalem, where he had been going for many years. This is despite him having with him various medical reports that show that his medical condition was critical and instead of him being allowed to go to his Medical Centre, the Occupation Forces started pushing and beating him until he was killed.

He was transferred after his martyrdom to a nearby medical centre, an Israeli Health Ministry Medical

Centre, who issued a report issued that confirms that Martyr Shehadeh died as a result of beating and injuries. This was obvious from the injuries on his head.

But the Occupation forces tried to deny responsibility as usual, just as they claimed today that the family of Huda Abu Ghalia, who were martyred on the Gaza beach a few days ago, were killed by a mine that the Palestinians planted. This is despite that more than one human rights and medical centre issued reports that confirms that the casualties were due to the Israeli shells, and despite the films that showed the Israeli shelling of the beach and the family.

Friends, our road for freedom is long and hard but what makes our life easier and gives us a boost is the fact that there are many friends and sympathisers all over the world. We in Abu Dis regard our close and special relationship with our friends in Camden a major and important source for our support and showing our suffering and what we are subjected to every second of our lives to the public opinion in Britain and the world.

In the hope that the increase in international public awareness about what is happening in our midst will increase the pressure on the occupation forces to come back to its senses and comply with the international law. And asking the Occupation to listen to the will of the international law, to its demand from the Occupation to recognise our people's national rights, which will be achieved sooner or later regardless of the sacrifices.

Friends, warm greetings from Abu Dis, and the family of Martyr Shehadeh. We shake hands strongly with you.

We value your interest and your warm condolences to Abu Dis and the family of the Martyr.

We hope you will stay in touch and we will work together to achieve freedom for all the peoples of the world, and the end of all forms of occupation and repression in the world.

Wishing you peace.

Further information

How the wider Palestinian issues relate to Abu Dis

Refugees

Since its beginning in 1948, Israel has pushed Palestinians to leave their land in the areas under Israeli control, and despite international law demanding the right for refugees to return, they have not allowed them to do so. There are currently an estimated six million Palestinians in the diaspora, most refugees in fact although not all registered as such. The stories of Palestinian people being prevented from returning to their country continue all the time, but there have been two huge waves of refugees. Abu Dis and area houses refugees from the first of these, and itself lost refugees in the second wave.

In 1947-8, there were huge pressures on Palestinians in villages and towns in the west of Palestine to leave. The Zionist armies pushed people from their homes by force: "Half of the indigenous people living in Palestine were driven out, half of their villages and towns were destroyed, and only very few among them ever managed to return.

From 1948 onwards, an unknown number of people tried to return but many were shot or disappeared at the borders.

Many refugees, mainly from West Jerusalem and its villages came at this time to Abu Dis and area – and to all areas of the West Bank, Gaza and adjacent countries. Because of the hilly ground of Abu Dis, this was not an area for a refugee camp. Families lived separately in places they could find, often beginning in the caves in the hills, and then moving into the town.

The refugee community now spans four generations. By 2003 in Abu Dis there were 1100 refugees from 250 families [5]. There are many more refugees in the area as a whole – Aizariyeh, to the north of Abu Dis has a refugee camp and Sawahreh to the south also has refugees. Abu Dis houses the UNWRA school for the children of these refugees.

The occupation in 1967 created many more refugees. Abu Dis found itself in the front line, and so about two-thirds of the people of Abu Dis left the town for the security of their families, often going first to local caves for shelter, then

east to the countryside, and on to Jericho and Jordan.

Just as in 1948, when Israel had allowed passage east but not west, so in 1967: Israel was not happy to let the Palestinians return. When the fighting stopped, the border was rapidly closed by Israel and many thousands found themselves refugees like the people of 1948, hoping and waiting to return.

A further group of people suddenly found themselves refugees in 1967. People who had been out of the West Bank and Gaza in June were not allowed to return. This applied to many thousands of students studying abroad, and to people working in Jordan or the Gulf. In 1967, from all these reasons, Abu Dis lost an estimated two-thirds of its population.

Land confiscation and settlements

Under the UN Partition Plan agreed in resolution 181 on 29th November 1947[1] the area round Jerusalem, including Abu Dis, was to be considered as an international area. At that point, Jerusalem, including Bethlehem, Ramallah, Abu Dis and the other suburbs, had an area of just over 70 km sq. Abu Dis itself had 30 000 donums of land (about 60 km sq) which stretched right back to the Dead Sea and in the direction of Jericho; not all of this was to be within the international zone.

This resolution was not brought into effect because following the 1948 war, Israel declared its state on a larger area of Palestine, including West Jerusalem. The upland area in the east of Palestine that Israel did not take came to be known as the West Bank (of the Jordan river) and Abu Dis was here; this area came under Jordanian rule.

In 1967, the whole of the West Bank was occupied by Israel. The first thing that happened to the land was the annexation of Jerusalem. This included some parts of western Abu Dis, the areas of Um Zarazeer and Kubsah.

Then from the 1970s, Israel began to take land over under military orders, much of this to build new towns for Israeli settlers. This is in direct contradiction to international law[2] but despite international resolutions calling for the movement to stop, it has escalated constantly.

After the Camp David peace agreement between Israel and Egypt, there was an organised policy of confiscation of Palestinian lands in the West Bank and Gaza Strip. The number of Israeli settlers in the West Bank grew constantly between 1975 and 1993, and then it doubled after the Oslo agreement between 1993 and 2000 – and by this time more than fifty percent of the West Bank land had been confiscated.

By now (2008), Israel has taken over about 60% of the West Bank from the Palestinians. Between East Jerusalem and the Dead Sea, approximately 80% of the land has been taken for military closed areas.

Around Abu Dis, land has been taken for the Maale Adumim settlement, which together with the settlements around it (Qidar, Mishor Adumim etc) has become one of the giant settlement blocs of the West Bank. Land has been taken for roads, a rubbish area, a new village for Bedouin that Israel wants to move from elsewhere, and for many military areas. This land includes areas within Abu Dis itself – taken for a military camp to control the area – as well as much agricultural land. Then from 2002, Israel started to confiscate swathes of land for the Separation Wall. Land confiscation is continuing up to today with large areas taken just before the Annapolis talks at the end of 2007.[3]

The Separation Wall

Abu Dis is a suburb of Jerusalem and in the past, before the Wall, Jerusalem and Abu Dis used to be the same community. People in Abu Dis used to go to Jerusalem daily, to their work in Jerusalem, to their hospital, for their education, to the main market, to the holy places, for entertainment, and it was the centre of their lives.

At the end of 2002 Israel started to build a wall between the people on the east side of the city and their city centre. First they blocked the roads and put in temporary barriers. For several years, Abu Dis people, old, young, fit and unwell had to go to Jerusalem by finding ways round the Wall – through gaps, watching out for soldiers, or by climbing and jumping low parts of the Wall.

This rapidly became impossible. The Wall was completed and the Israelis built huge checkpoints in it, like international frontiers, which became the only way through. As a result there are now around 70,000 people in the East Jerusalem suburbs who are almost completely isolated. They have lost their opportunity to reach Jerusalem, and it is also very hard for them to travel to the rest of the West Bank because of the Wall, military checkpoints, and no-go areas for Palestinians such as Israeli bypass roads, settlements and military areas.

The whole area is now controlled by Israeli military camps. In Abu Dis there are two of them – one on the east side of Abu Dis and one inside Abu Dis on the west side – and the major settlements that have taken over the lands on both the east and the west of the East Jerusalem suburbs.

Following the Oslo agreement and the creation of the Palestinian Authority, the West Bank was divided into areas A (Palestinian policing), C (full Israeli control) and B (between the two). Abu Dis has parts in B and parts in C – so it does not come under the control of the Palestinian Authority. Israel has also declared Jerusalem as part of Israel (this does not have international recognition) and extended the municipal boundaries of Jerusalem.

This appears to create a complex situation, and certainly sometimes it is obviously contradictory – some people in Abu Dis are on the east of the Wall but the west of the Jerusalem municipal boundary: they are required to pay high Jerusalem taxes but are not given any services and not allowed into Jerusalem.

Similarly, the route of the Wall on first sight appears to meander in a haphazard fashion across the West Bank, deep inside it and far beyond the Green Line – the 1948 ceasefire line that the international community has for years accepted as the Israel-Palestine border.

However, the route of the Wall is not haphazard, and there is a logic to the Wall. It is being built close up against the Palestinian communities and across their land, in such a way that it can be possible to loop the Israeli settlements, their roads and the major aquifers of the West Bank back into association with Israel, together with the maximum possible land around the settlements.

This entraps the Palestinians in tiny spaces, upsetting the economy, constricting the people and making it very difficult for them to leave a normal life. They argue that the reason for this is an Israeli attempt not only to take over their land, but to force the Palestinian people to leave.

In 2004, the International Court of Justice in the Hague found the Wall to be illegal – see Appendix 4.

Israeli checkpoints

Since the Israelis started to build the Separation Wall around Jerusalem they have worked to seal off Jerusalem very thoroughly from its suburb. The ways into Jerusalem separate people by their type of pass. For the towns near Abu Dis on the east of Jerusalem, there are two main ways into Jerusalem.

People with Jerusalem passes can use the checkpoint at Al-Zayem, on the Jerusalem road leading to the settlement of Maale Adumim, and here (for people with the right sort of pass) it is possible to drive through the checkpoint.

Al-Zeituna terminal, between the Mount of Olives and the town of Aizariyeh, is for people carrying West Bank passes and who also have managed to obtain a permit. Here there are very long and complicated procedures, especially now that they use fingerprints as well as permits.

If people without Jerusalem residence want to go to Jerusalem, they first have to go to the Civil Department to apply for a permit and they may or may not be given one, even if (for example) they have a doctor's letter to refer them to one of the Jerusalem hospitals. It is also the case that even with a permit, sometimes people are prevented from going through to Jerusalem. This is very serious for example in the case of health treatment – all the local hospitals for Abu Dis are in Jerusalem. Abu Dis doctors have estimated that only about two-thirds of people given referral letters to Jerusalem hospitals are actually able to reach the hospital.

If they manage to get a permit to go to Jerusalem, Palestinians now have to go through special 'terminals' very like international frontiers. People are not allowed to drive. There is a system of metal turnstiles and electronic gates and checks that involve people especially in mornings and evenings in big crowds, long queues and waits that can be for hours. It is a very humiliating experience, even when people are not singled out – as they frequently are- for more intensive checks. The terminals separate the Israeli soldiers from the Palestinians behind thick glass, and they shout orders to them over loudspeakers in Hebrew (which is not the local language).

The East Jerusalem towns are surrounded by checkpoints in all directions. To go to Bethlehem in the south, people from Abu Dis have to go through the Container checkpoint. And it is not always possible to reach Ramallah from Abu Dis because of fixed checkpoints at Jabaa and 'flying' (temporary) checkpoints that can be anywhere. There is a checkpoint on the road to Jericho.

The situation is unpredictable: Palestinians are told that they will entirely be banned from some of these roads in the near future, but in the meantime, the checkpoints are often closed without notice for supposed security reasons or for Jewish religious holidays, entirely paralysing the area.

Within Abu Dis itself, the army often puts up flying checkpoints, particularly on the main road to the university and near the schools. Here young people

in particular are often held up for hours, stood against walls, waiting for their IDs to be returned, and are sometimes beaten or arrested.

Israeli pass laws and the issue of Jerusalem citizenship

There has been tremendous pressure on Palestinians in East Jerusalem since 1967. Following its occupation of the West Bank, Israel immediately annexed Jerusalem, treating it differently from the rest of the West Bank. Then began an effort on their part to build up the number of Jewish settlers and displace the Palestinians from the East part of the city.

Throughout this period, Israeli take-overs of Palestinian houses and entire neighbourhoods in Jerusalem, the construction of Israeli settlements and the destruction of Palestinian houses have gone alongside efforts to reduce the percentage of Palestinians in Jerusalem to under 28 percent.

Following the annexation of the city by Israel, Palestinians from East Jerusalem were given residency but Israel did not want the Palestinian Jerusalemites to become full citizens of Israel – they do not, for example, have a vote in the Knesset.

At first, it was a liability to have a Palestinian Jerusalem ID – it meant paying more taxes (income tax to Israel as well as the Jerusalem arnona) and for Jerusalem residents (Palestinian) it was not possible to get a licence to build.. But progressively from 1991, the Jerusalem ID has given its holders more freedom than the West Bank ID-holders, and very importantly it has become the key to being allowed to go to Jerusalem, as well as to live there.

In recent years, the Israeli effort to reduce the number of Palestinians in Jerusalem has increased. Since 1967 it has been nearly impossible for Palestinians with West Bank IDs to get a Jerusalem ID; and a law was passed in 2002 stating explicitly that Palestinians with Jerusalem residency or with Israeli passports may not bring their Palestinian spouses with West Bank IDs to live in Jerusalem or Israel..

After the building of the Wall, many Jerusalemites who had moved into the suburbs have moved back to live inside the city, and Palestinians still represent 35 percent of the population of Jerusalem city itself. This has led to further efforts on the part of the Israeli authorities to reduce the number of Palestinians in the city and constant checking and questioning of the IDs of Jerusalem Palestinians. Five thousand Palestinian families have lost their IDs since 1973 and in the space of just one year 2006, after Israel had separated Jerusalem completely from its suburbs, 1,363 Jerusalem residents lost their Jerusalem IDs.

This is a major issue for people in and around Abu Dis. Most people in Abu Dis have West Bank IDs but many people who have Jerusalem IDs live in these suburbs. An estimated 800 married couples have mixed IDs and either have to live apart or cope with a very real threat of separation.

In an average month during the past two years there have been about 75 prisoners from Abu Dis town in Israeli jails, and among them between 20 and 25 children at any one time. In addition there have usually been an average of about 70 students from Al Quds University Abu Dis campus in prison.

There are huge issues about the ways that prisoners have been treated. They are are tried (if at all) by military courts, in Hebrew. (Palestinian prisoners in Israeli jails include many imprisoned with no trial. The Israelis call this administrative detention.) Israeli has not treated the young people as juveniles. Many prisoners have suffered bad treatment, physical and psychological torture, and had confessions forced from them. An enormous issue for prisoners and their families is denial of family visits.

There is further information on the situation in Abu Dis at **www.camdenabudis.net**

Mass imprisonment

Since the beginning of the Occupation, the Israeli authorities have had a policy of invading houses and arresting Palestinians. This has amounted to a policy of mass imprisonment which over the years of the Occupation has affected many thousands of men in Palestine and hundreds of women.

In Abu Dis, just as in the rest of Palestine, hundreds of people from Abu Dis have been arrested, usually for peaceful resistance against the Occupation, such as demonstrations; and among these there have been many young people under the age of eighteen.

FOOTNOTES

[1] Since then, 29th November has been the International Day of Solidarity with the Palestinian People

[2] Part 49 of the 4th Geneva Convention – international human rights law

[3] CADFA human rights report October 2007 and February 2008, see www.camdenabudis.net

Why do they call it apartheid?

This book consists of contributions that people from Abu Dis have sent to us in Camden, telling us about their lives. But in four years one subject has not been covered by letters they have sent.

We have now organised dozens of visits from Abu Dis to Camden and vice versa, and dozens of public meetings in Camden discussing the issues, and we have realised that there is something important but so obvious to people in Abu Dis that they often don't explain it, and that remains so unclear in Camden, that we need to add a note ourselves.

The issue that is missing is the huge separation between Palestinian and Israeli people in Palestine. Palestinians don't describe it in their letters to us, because it is to them completely obvious: the Israelis who arrived in Palestine as military occupiers are not interested in living together with the Palestinians, but in taking over the land.

Some people talk about the situation in Palestine as 'apartheid,' which is a reference to the system of rigid ethnic separation in South Africa (1949-91) though others argue with the title. We will leave the reader to decide if the label is important, but we need to explain why it is used.

In Camden we are sometimes asked questions like whether Palestinian children have the chance to meet Israeli children; and we sometimes notice, when people come from Abu Dis, that they will tell of 'settlements' and that people in Camden don't really understand what they are. These are a few of the things that you would find on a visit to Palestine:

The West Bank and Gaza were taken by military force by Israel in 1967. They are still under military rule.

There are international laws (the Geneva accords) that prohibit the settlement of occupied land by the occupying power. Nevertheless, there has been a huge take-over of Palestinian land and rapid building of new towns in the West Bank and, until 2005, in Gaza.

These Israeli 'settlements' are new towns specifically for Jews, not for people to live in together. There have been big efforts including government subsidies

NANDITA DOWSON, 2008

to persuade Israelis to live there, and many of the settlers are not originally Israeli at all, but are from the United States, Russia or elsewhere and encouraged by the Israeli Law of Return.

Palestinian refugees from 1948, 1967 and from all many deportations in between have not been allowed to return to Palestine, with the exception of some families with links to the Palestinian authority who were allowed to come back after the Oslo agreement of 1993.

Palestinians living locally have been brought in to the settlements as labourers or else as prisoners (for example, young men from Abu Dis often see the inside of Maale Adumim police station) but they are not otherwise allowed to go there, and they certainly cannot live there.

The settlements are military points, built usually on hilltops, fortified and guarded. Settlers are often armed, and there are many incidents of settler violence against local Palestinians, particularly where the settlement is trying to expand.

The facilities available to the settlements and to the Palestinian towns and villages are dramatically different. The settlements consist of Western-style housing, and have more electricity, more water, swift access on modern roads to Jerusalem. The Palestinian towns, villages and refugee camps are often in great hardship. The contrasts between the educational resources for the two groups of children are dramatic.

People living in the settlements and in the towns have a separate road system. The smooth settlement bypass roads link the settlements and Israel. The poor-quality Palestinian roads are blocked intermittently by checkpoints, and efforts are being made to create tunnels and bridges to ensure that the two road systems, already largely separate, are completely apart.

There is clear discrimination between Israelis and Palestinians in all Israeli rulings, from building regulations (Israelis can build in the West Bank. under Israeli law, if not under international law – but

Palestinians do not get planning permission and often have their new buildings demolished) to water wells (Israelis can draw off certain levels of the water table, and Palestinians must go elsewhere).

Israelis in the settlements are on Palestinian land, but they and the Palestinians next door are judged by completely separate laws. A settler in trouble with the law is judged by Israeli civil law and civil courts. Palestinians are living under another set of rules. Following the Oslo agreement of 1993, Palestinians in the West Bank may be in an Area A, Area B or Area C. In Area A, there are Palestinian police. But in Areas B and C, there is no civil law for Palestinians, and all problems between people have to be sorted out between themselves by family networks and local people.

Much more likely for Palestinians, in all these areas, is a problem with the Israeli army which has a policy of military arrests. This often brings local children as well as young adults into military courts, where they are tried in a language that is foreign to them. Palestinians are judged as adult at 16, where Israelis judge their own to be juvenile until 18.

Israelis living in settlements have a vote in the Israeli Knesset elections. Palestinians have a vote for the Palestinian authority, although in fact the outside world determines whether the results of the election are acceptable, as the Palestinians discovered when they were punished by sanctions for their votes in January 2006. But the Israeli government is the one that controls the military, the settlement policy, the laws. So there is an ethnic division here too: Israelis living on Palestinian lands have a vote, but the Palestinians have no say in the government that determines their lives.

So, do Israeli and Palestinian children play together? No, Palestinian children meet Israeli adults in their army uniforms. They see cars sweeping Israeli families by on their separate fenced roads. They suffer from the occupation and sometimes directly from the settlers. But the children do not meet.

Haiku: on Israel's sixty years celebration

Written by a poet in a Jewish group protesting at Israel's celebrations of sixty years

Across the West Bank

Jabotinsky's Iron Wall

makes itself concrete.

Smooth West Bank highway;

we can drive without seeing

a single Arab.

Unilateral –

the sound of one hand clapping;

Israel's art of Zen.

DEBORAH MACCOBY 2008

Resources

Shrinking Palestine

1917
PALESTINE
- Haifa
- Jaffa
- Jerusalem
- Gaza

River Jordan

Dead Sea

EGYPT

Jews own **2.5%** of land

20 miles

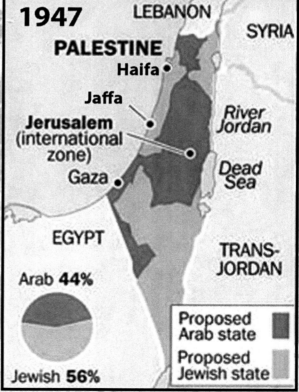

1947
LEBANON

SYRIA

PALESTINE
- Haifa
- Jaffa
- **Jerusalem** (international zone)
- Gaza

River Jordan

Dead Sea

EGYPT

TRANS-JORDAN

Arab **44%**

Jewish **56%**

Proposed Arab state

Proposed Jewish state

1948-1967

LEBANON

SYRIA

ISRAEL

Tel Aviv

River Jordan

Jerusalem (Divided)

Gaza

GAZA STRIP Occupied by Egypt

WEST BANK occupied by Jordan

Arab **22%**

JORDAN

EGYPT

Israel **78%**

20 miles

1967

LEBANON

SYRIA Golan Heights occ. by Israel

ISRAEL

Tel Aviv

River Jordan

Jerusalem

Gaza

GAZA STRIP Occupied by Israel

WEST BANK Occupied by Israel

Sinai Occupied by Israel, later returned

Since 1967, all of Palestine has been under Israeli control

20 miles

How the West Bank has been fragmented

2008

LEBANON SYRIA

ISRAEL

Golan Heights (occ. by Israel)

Tel Aviv

Jerusalem

Gaza

GAZA STRIP occupied by Israel (settlements removed in 2005)

WEST BANK occupied by Israel

JORDAN

20 miles

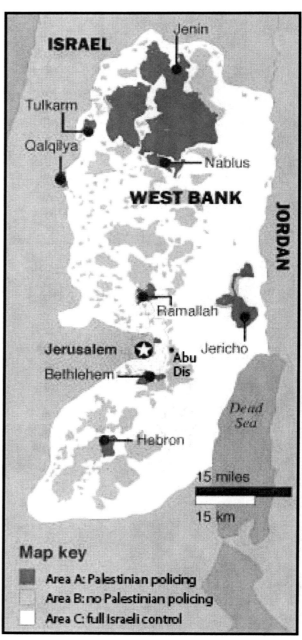

ISRAEL

Jenin

Tulkarm

Qalqilya

Nablus

WEST BANK

JORDAN

Ramallah

Jerusalem

Bethlehem

Abu Dis

Jericho

Dead Sea

Hebron

15 miles

15 km

Map key

Area A: Palestinian policing

Area B: no Palestinian policing

Area C: full Israeli control

The Wall

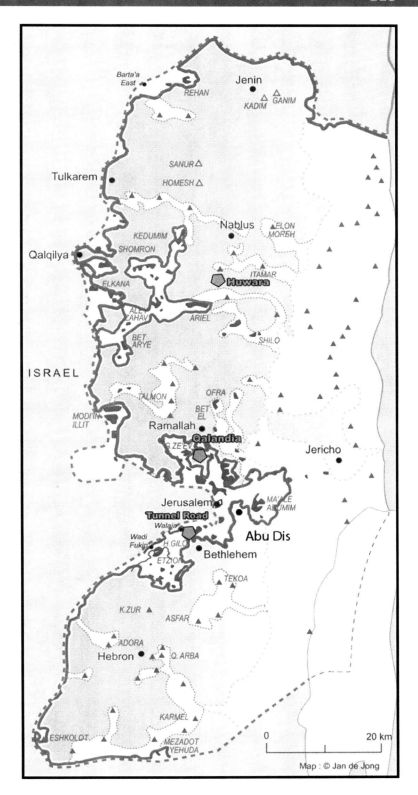

Map : © Jan de Jong

This map shows the route of the Wall through the West Bank, running close to Palestinian towns and villages, and cutting away empty land and water resources, and leaving the main settlements linked by 'bypass roads' to Israel

The map includes some of the Israeli settlements and just a few of the military checkpoints in existence in 2008. For good maps showing checkpoints and settlements, see the following United Nations website: www.ochaopt.org – look for Map Centre

For more maps of Palestine, see www.passia.org

The area around Abu Dis

Abu Dis is now cut off by the Wall from the centre of Jerusalem

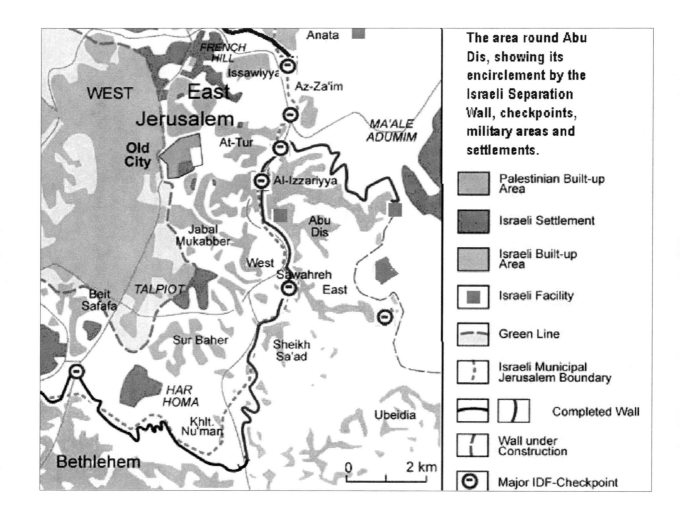

The area round Abu Dis, showing its encirclement by the Israeli Separation Wall, checkpoints, military areas and settlements.

Palestinian Built-up Area	
Israeli Settlement	
Israeli Built-up Area	
Israeli Facility	
Green Line	
Israeli Municipal Jerusalem Boundary	
Completed Wall	
Wall under Construction	
Major IDF-Checkpoint	

Map labels: Anata, FRENCH HILL, Issawiyya, Az-Za'im, WEST, East Jerusalem, MA'ALE ADUMIM, Old City, At-Tur, Al-Izzariyya, Jabal Mukabber, Abu Dis, West Sawahreh East, Beit Safafa, TALPIOT, Sur Baher, Sheikh Sa'ad, HAR HOMA, Khlt. Nu'man, Ubeidia, Bethlehem

0   2 km

Palestine and Abu Dis timeline

4 centuries till 1918	Palestine was under Turkish rule	In Abu Dis, people talk about the misery that people lived under under the Turkish rule, used to be forced to join the army, used to be arrested from their houses.
1897	First Zionist Congress	Taxes from the Turkish rulers were one reason why the people lost their land. Legal papers started to be used which did not show that they and their families had been cultivating the land for centuries. The Turkish demanded ushur (like a tithe) from people, and if this could not be paid, the Turkish officials came to the houses to remove all they could find.
		People had such problems with the tax that they often either registered either only the land that was barren (with lower tax) or a small part in the centre of their land, to protect their own land and reduce the amount of tax. Big areas of good agricultural land that were still being used had no apparent legal owner.
		While the Turks were still there, this did not always get noticed. This land came to be known as Emiri (state). The files were passed to the British, then the Jordanians, then the Israelis, and now some of the land that the settlements are built on is this land.
		Under the Turkish rules, there were good relations between the Palestinian Jews and Abu Dis people. There was a cheese factory owned by Palestinian Jews in Abu Dis.
		Problems started in 1917 when the Zionist Foundation for Land started to buy land in Abu Dis. Before that, the relation between Muslims, Jews and Christians was good. They used to buy land from each other. But when the Zionist Foundation started to buy land in Abu Dis under the British authority, there were a lot of problems – OFTEN THROUGH AN AGENT WHO BOUGHT IT ON BEHALF OF THEM.
		The Zionist Foundation, supported famously in Abu Dis and Jerusalem by the money of a Russian millionaire Moscovitch, bought land from absentee landlords. Previously land had changed ownership at the level of absentee landlords often but the people who had always lived and worked on it continued to do so. However now, the Zionists started to turn the people off their land or tell them what to do with it.
		After 1918 there were people from Abu Dis arrested by the British because they refused to pass their land to the Zionist Foundation or to have its use changed, for example to have roads built on it for the Zionists.
		Once someone from Abu Dis shot at a representative of the Zionist Foundation.

1914-18	First world war	During the Turkish period, the Turkish used to come to the village to collect men between 16 and 40 and take them by force to join the army – the were taken to different fronts and many were lost in Egypt, Cyprus, Yemen on different fronts. In 1917, the British put their tanks where the Abu Dis graveyard now is, and shot east towards Turkish positions.
1916	Arab revolution against the Turks encouraged by British promises of independence for the Arab nations following defeat of the Turks	Some people in Abu Dis were fighting alongside the Turkish against the British and some (under the flag of the Arab Revolution) were fighting alongside the British against the Turkish. This divided Abu Dis itself. People on both sides were arrested and killed
1916	Sykes-Picot Agreement: Britain and France agreed on division of control of middle east between them, with Palestine under British control	
1917	Balfour Declaration promises Jews a homeland in Palestine	
1918	British control over Palestine following end of first world war	1919 Thowrat al-Buraq in Jerusalem area. Uprising arising from conflicts between Palestinians and Jews in the area of Al Buraq Square (now become the Wailing Wall Plaza). Many Abu Dis people were wounded.
1922	British Mandate in Palestine under leadership of Zionist Herbert Samuel.	
	Zionist immigration to Palestine increasing	
1927		Earthquake in Palestine, which destroyed most of the houses in Abu Dis
1929	Palestinian rebellion	

1936–9	Qassam rebellion (Palestinian rebellion)	Many people from Abu Dis were arrested and tortured by the British. One Abu Dis man was person involved in a military action against the British intelligence officer (called Moses) who was in charge of Abu Dis.
1939-45	Second world war	Abu Dis people were asked by the British to put up blackout as the Germans bombed Haifa, Jaffa etc.
		1945-46 the British besieged Abu Dis. They put a checkpoint at Kubsa. They went in for collective punishment such as calling the whole village out to the cemetery, or making everyone go in to their houses, or making them mix their supplies of oil into their flour.
		1945, Abu Dis people created four fighting units to fight against the British Mandate and the Zionist movement. These units were joined to the Jordanian army in 1948
		In 1946, the Halabiyeh area of Abu Dis was bombed by the British.
29th Nov 1947	UN Partition Plan	UN Partition plan put Abu Dis, Bethlehem and Ramallah along with Jerusalem into the international area
1947-8	Israeli terror groups attacking Palestinian civilians; some Palestinian armed resistance

1945 British emergency law said that any Palestinian found with even a bullet would be executed. | 1947 Jerusalem, 3 women from Abu Dis were killed by bomb at Damascus Gate, Jerusalem

In 1947, Ahmad Rabiya, a fighter from Abu Dis, was shot by the British at Latron

Two Abu Dis men were executed by the British under this law. |
| 1948 | April – Deir Yassin Massacre; many other massacres and attacks on towns;

May -Arab-Israeli War

Nakba – vast exodus of refugees | Refugees from 1948 Palestine came to Abu Dis (as well as the rest of the region)

Abu Dis came under Jordanian rule as part of the "West Bank" |

1950	Jericho conference announced union between Jordan and the West Bank.	Kamel Eriqat from Abu Dis was part of the conference. After this, many Abu Dis men got work in the Jordanian army.
Mid-1950s	Many Palestinian men went to work in the Gulf, specially Kuwait, and to America.	1955 Abu Ali Eriqat, Abu Mousa Al Baow, Abu Yousef Bader: Three men from Abu Dis went walking to Kuwait walking and lost their way in the desert – found by a police officer in the army saying what had happened to them saying they were dying of thirst
		In a factory in one of the Abu Dis caves, people made palm mats and sold them all over Palestine – showing the connection between Abu Dis people and their land by Dead Sea, which is where the raw materials came from
1960	Idea of creating a college for Jerusalem came from Kuwait. The Kuwaiti Government announced that they were ready to build the college if anyone would donate the land.	Everything was organised through the families. General meeting in Abu Dis gave 190 donums from different families, and they sent a delegation to Kuwait to register the land in the name of the college. They thought this would be able to change something in the lives of Abu Dis. 1960 Start of a cigarette factory in Abu Dis although there was pressure from the Jordanian king to have the factory on the east side of the river. There was a meeting with the people who wanted to build the factory (Alami family) together with Abu Dis people, who helped them to start their project in Abu Dis
1967	Naksa and the occupation of the rest of Palestine Israelis announced the decision to annexe East Jerusalem (not recognised internationally)	Abu Dis was occupied by Israel, many refugees left to Jordan, many people killed. The majority of refugees have not been allowed to return Land expropriation started in East Jerusalem, the West Bank and Gaza.
1968	Battle of Karameh – Israel crossed the Jordan river (to the east) but was defeated	

1970	Black September – PLO-Jordanian struggle, PLO left Jordan	Abu Dis Water Society started.
1973	October War (Israel: Syria & Egypt)	Abu Dis people were asked by Israeli loudspeakers to paint their glass blue (blackout)
1976	Land Day: Protests over Israeli seizure of Palestinian land	Israelis started building the settlement of Maale Adumim. Big demonstrations in Abu Dis. Ali Afaneh (boy from Abu Dis) shot by Israeli army.
1979	Settlement building continuing, increasing	Curfew on Abu Dis lasted a complete month; 2 people from Abu Dis killed by Israeli army; two houses destroyed by the Israeli army The Al Quds College started to work in 1979 with 600 students.
1980		Mishor Adumim settlement started
1981		Political parties started public work in Abu Dis.
1982	Israeli invasion of Lebanon	Curfew and demonstrations in Abu Dis Strike in Al Golan – people from Abu Dis prepared food and took it to Al Golan
1983		First democratic elections for Water Society, candidates from parties not families
1985	As a result of political work in Palestine, Israel announced Iron Fist policy - giving administrative detention to those involved in public political work in the West Bank.	Qidar settlement started Six people from Abu Dis put in administrative detention (out of 100 from the whole of the West Bank and Gaza Strip)

1987	First intifada started	5 people from Abu Dis killed by the Israeli army
		In July, a decision in the Israeli Knesset to join Abu Dis to Jerusalem.
		August, demonstrations in Abu Dis and five people wounded att the starting of the first intifada.
		29th September 2000 – Bilal Afaneh First shaheed in second intifada, killed in the Al Aqsa Mosque. Youth in Abu Dis active in the first intifada - Israeli police station burned, Eged bus burned
		First announcement from the Palestinian general commander was printed and published in Abu Dis – Mohammed al Labady – since deported from Palestine.
		In December 1987, the Israelis shut the media out of Abu Dis
1991	First Gulf War	
1993	Oslo Accords, establishment of Palestinian Authority	Division of West Bank into Areas A, B, C: Abu Dis put in areas B and C
1996	Intifada in protest against Israel opening a tunnel under the Al Aqsa Mosque	Curfew and demonstrations in Abu Dis
1998	Prisoners' uprising	Nasser Eriqat killed by Israelis in Abu Dis
2000	Israelis withdrew from South Lebanon and took their tanks to the West Bank	
	Second Intifada (Al Aqsa Intifada)	6 people from Abu Dis killed by the Israeli army

2002	Massacres in Jenin and in Nablus Israel started building the Wall in the north of the West Bank	
2003		Israel started the Wall in Abu Dis
2005	Israel withdrew from some settlements in Gaza but continued to control its borders, overfly with military aircraft and bombard	
2006		Israel completed closure of all the ways to Jerusalem from Abu Dis; new terminals in place
2007		Major land expropriation in Abu Dis

Excerpts from the Universal Declaration of Human Rights, 1948

You can find the full statement at
www.unhchr.ch/udhr/

Eleanor Roosevelt holding the Universal Declaration of Human Rights

From the preamble:

"... disregard and contempt for human rights have resulted in barbarous acts which have outraged the conscience of mankind..."

Note that the Universal Declaration calls for these rights for

"Everyone... without distinction of any kind, such as race, colour, sex, language, religion, political or other opinion, national or social origin, property, birth or other status..."

Human rights include the following:

- Everyone has the right to life, liberty and security of person. (article 3)

- No one shall be subjected to torture or to cruel, inhuman or degrading treatment or punishment. (article 5)

- All are equal before the law and are entitled without any discrimination to equal protection of the law. (article 7)

- No one shall be subjected to arbitrary arrest, detention or exile. (article 9)

- No one shall be subjected to arbitrary interference with his privacy, family, home or correspondence, nor to attacks upon his honour and reputation. (article 12)

- Everyone has the right to freedom of movement and residence within the borders of each State.

- Everyone has the right to leave any country, including his own, and to return to his country. (article 13)

- The family is the natural and fundamental group unit of society and is entitled to protection by society and the State. (article 16-3)

- Motherhood and childhood are entitled to special care and assistance. All children, whether born in or out of wedlock, shall enjoy the same social protection. (Article 25–2)

- No one shall be arbitrarily deprived of his property. (article 17-2)

- Everyone has the right to take part in the government of his country, directly or through freely chosen representatives… The will of the people shall be the basis of the authority of government;. (Article 21–1,3)

- Everyone has the right to education. (article 26–1)

2004 Judgment against the Separation Wall

In July 2004 the **International Court of Justice** in The Hague gave its opinion on the legality of the Wall.

They said the Wall is illegal because:

- it is an annexation of Palestinian land which violates the Palestinian right to self-determination

- It is a breach of international humanitarian law in the fourth Geneva Convention, which applies in the occupied territories, because:

- it is intended to assist settlements and the settlements violate Article 49 of the Convention

- restrictions placed on Palestinians between the wall and the Green Line violate Article 49

- taking control of private land to build the wall violates Articles 46 and 52 of the Hague regulations of 1907 and Article 53 of the Geneva Convention

- It is a breach of international human rights law which, the Court said, applies in its entirety in the occupied territory. In particular the Court said that the wall:

- Breaches rights to freedom of movement

- Breaches the rights to privacy and the right to family

- Breaches the right to work

- Breaches the right to an adequate standard of living, health and education

The ICJ said that Israel must:

- Stop building the Wall

- Dismantle the Wall built inside the West Bank

- Revoke the Orders to construct the Wall

- Compensate the Palestinians affected by the Wall

The ICJ called on the international community to:

- refrain from assisting the unlawful situation created by the Wall

- take legal measures to stop Israel's violation of international law

- ensure enforcement of the Fourth Geneva Convention

Where to find more information

THERE IS LOTS OF INFORMATION ON THE INTERNET AND USEFUL BOOKS AND FILMS. HERE ARE SOME GOOD PLACES TO START.

The history

Avi Shlaim: "The Iron Wall"
Film: "Jerusalem: the East Side Story"

Old Palestine and refugees

www.palestineremembered.com
Ilan Pappe: "The Ethnic Cleansing of Palestine"
Film: Route 181

The Wall

www.stopthewall.org
Film: The Iron Wall

Human rights and international humanitarian law

www.alhaq.org/
www.diakonia.se/sa/site.asp?site=777
United Nations Office for the Co-ordination of Humanitarian Affairs (very useful reports and maps)
www.ochaopt.org/

Situation of children

www.dci-pal.org

Children's story

" A Little Piece of Ground" Elizabeth Laird (and Sonia Nimr)

Abu Dis

Oral history from 1967: Eds N Dowson and A W Sabbah, "The First Six Days" (CADFA)

Films from CADFA Youth Film Project 2008: "The New Map of Abu Dis", "The Great Wall of Palestine"

CADFA's work:

N. Dowson "Makloubeh, or Facts on the Ground" (2005) (CADFA)

www.camdenabudis.net

CADFA are happy to provide speakers, exhibitions, films for schools and other groups in Camden (or to help twinning groups across the country)

Note on the work of Camden Abu Dis Friendship Association

"This is the first time we find someone who supports us in what we ask for, not according to themselves or their countries' political agendas." (from Abu Dis)

CADFA works to promote human rights and respect for international humanitarian law in Palestine. We currently work in the following areas:

- Information (publications, public meetings, our website www.camdenabudis.net)

- Visits and volunteers (visits from Camden to Abu Dis and visits from Abu Dis to Camden; volunteers going to Abu Dis to work in a number of projects including English language teaching)

- Twinning projects (links between peers in Camden and Abu Dis, work together on positive projects in Abu Dis; current links groups include education, health, women, students)

- Campaigns (urgent action human rights campaigns and our on-going prisoner adoption campaign)

There is more information on our website
www.camdenabudis.net

We would welcome your help and support.

Printed in the United Kingdom
by Lightning Source UK Ltd.
135324UK00001B/197-346/P

9 780955 613616

Printed in the United Kingdom
by Lightning Source UK Ltd.
135324UK00001B/197-346/P